I0826386

Becoming...

Poetic Reflections Looking Back At It All

by

Dr. I. Joseph Care

Varun Pathak, Illustrations Editor

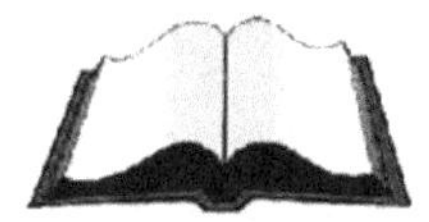

CCB Publishing
British Columbia, Canada

Becoming... : Poetic Reflections Looking Back At It All

ISBN-13: 978-1-77143-418-8
First Edition

Library and Archives Canada Cataloguing in Publication
Title: Becoming... : poetic reflections looking back at it all
/ by Dr. I. Joseph Care ; Varun Pathak, illustrations editor.
Names: Care, I. Joseph, author. | Pathak, Varun, editor.
Identifiers: Canadiana 2020030450X | ISBN 9781771434188 (softcover)
Classification: LCC PS3603.A74 B43 2020 | DDC 811/.6—dc23

Disclaimer: This is a work of fiction. Names, places, and characters are a product of the author's imagination or are used fictitiously and are not to be considered as real. Resemblance to any events or persons, living or dead, past or present, is purely coincidental.

Extreme care has been taken by the author to ensure that all information presented in this book is accurate and up to date at the time of publishing. Neither the author nor the publisher can be held responsible for any errors or omissions. Additionally, neither is any liability assumed for damages resulting from the use of the information contained herein.

Dr. I. Joseph Care may be contacted through CCB Publishing at: info@ccbpublishing.com

Publisher: CCB Publishing
British Columbia, Canada
www.ccbpublishing.com

Preface

Becoming . . . : *Poetic Reflections Looking Back At It All* is an insightful collection of original poetic expressions that evolved over years of personal journal jottings. The array of topics reflects on a wide variety of life experiences and recognizes that *'becoming'* is a growth process involving choices, goals and opportunities.

Selections can be used to stimulate introspection, encourage extended writing and prompt meaningful discussion. This can assist individuals and support groups to focus on feelings, put them in perspective and help deal with them more clearly.

The poetic expressions are alphabetically organized by topic. Each extended piece has a concept definition and thought-provoking discussion themes. Creative illustrations enhance the varied topics.

May this expansive collection of expressive thoughts and intriguing illustrations be helpful to and enjoyed by all in the process of *'becoming.'*

Author's Note

The poetic expressions and images in the book are for readers to enjoy, contemplate and reflect on. By focusing on specific topics, readers can explore feelings and issues and gain perspective for dealing with the important process of *'becoming.'* Individual poems can be selected for extended discussion, writing and drawing. The material can also be discussed and shared in group settings.

What's in the book?

- Poetic expressions: - Alphabetically organized by topic
- Concept Definitions: - Before each extended piece
- Thoughts for Discussion: - After each extended piece
- Poetic Blurbs: - With check-off topic boxes
- Creative Illustrations: - For selected topics
- Contents Boxes: - For each alphabet section
- Appendix: - Alphabetical topic & page listing

Suggestions for extended use:

- Select relevant topics: - Topics are in alphabetical order
  Use Contents Page, Contents Boxes and Appendix
- Read individually: - Make notes, underline
- Read with others: - Take turns
- Read to others: - Be expressive
- Share: - React to what is read

Relate to personal experience:

- Write, Draw, Journal: - Explore feelings, thoughts

Appreciate the process:

- Allow yourself time to focus and reflect

CONTENTS: Sections - Pages

Acknowledgments:

All illustrations are the property of I. Care Creations, LLC.

Illustrators:

Anita M. Oakley: (33, *circa 1980)*

*Scanned and adjusted for clarity; *several modified*

Pp. 7, 9, 35, 44, 47, 51, 58, 61, 70, 72, 85, 88, 99, 105, 120, 133, 136, 145, 164, 187, 193, 207, 209, 211*, 214, 224, 228*, 237, 242, 250, 261, 263, 266

Christine Ramien: (5, *circa 1990)*

Pp. 12, 18, 76, 107, 188

Varun Pathak: (41 + COVER, *2020)*

Pp. 1, 16, 19, 25, 32, 39, 54, 56, 65, 71, 78, 93, 98, 109, 112, 125,127, 139, 142, 147, 155, 156, 159, 171, 172, 174, 177, 181, 189, 200, 204, 206, 211*, 216, 219, 220, 228*, 230, 235, 245, 248; C1

Editorial Review: B. Fine, B. Kaye

A *Pp. 1-15*

☐ abrasiveness

Abrasiveness
is irritating.

abrasiveness

ACCEPTANCE (n.) - willingness to receive

acceptance

Reality becomes frightening
 and expectations become frustrating
  if *'What Is'* isn't what you want it to be.

When acceptance of *'What Is'*
 crashes the psyche into a wall of reality,
only the brakes of truth
 and the seat belts of open eyes and ears
  can shield you from being immobilized
   and unable to move forward.

When you can accept *'What Is,'*
 then expectations can become realistic
  and hopes can become doable.

Openness to the support
 of caring and responsible passersby
  can help you pull together shattered pieces
   from the crash of past hopes and dreams
  and get you back on a reasonable road
   toward what can now actually be possible.

Thoughts: Hopes and dreams in context • Grief stages

☐ ache (n.)

If you make the ache,
 soothe the bruise.

☐ achievement

Where do we land in life?
 Where our achievements take us!

ACTOR (n.) - performer; not using genuine behavior

actor

A versatile actor on the stage of life
transforms an insatiable need to hide from reality
into a made-up fantasy world
in order to have purpose and get attention.

Eagerly accepting whatever role is requested,
he performs to satisfy the audience available
hoping to entice them to return for more.

He uses whatever techniques in his vast repertoire
that will capture, convince and win over those
who at first may not believe the act.

The performance is a created illusion.
What you see is not what you get;
but it is so convincing that
he begins to deceive himself.

The performance that is fantasy
gradually becomes his reality.

Thoughts: Be yourself • Fantasy vs. reality

☐addict

An addict: A grotesque quarterback
maneuvering his prized poison through
the gauntlet of caring blockers, and using
every deceitful tactic to avoid being stopped
from completing his destructive mission.

Source: See P. 64

☐addiction

Once you use,
you abuse!

AGES (n.) - stages of life

ages

Child

Arms:	To reach out and hug.
Feet:	To run to the safety and security of the familiar.
Mouth:	To kiss with feeling.
Hands:	To touch lovingly.
Eyes:	To look for those who care.
Feelings:	To wear openly for all to understand.

Teenager

Arms:	To keep others away.
Feet:	To run to the safety and security of isolation.
Mouth:	To keep closed so no one will know your thoughts.
Hands:	To explore cautiously.
Eyes:	To look out for others and avoid.
Feelings:	To mask and hide behind so others won't see.

Adult

Arms:	To keep others at a safe distance.
Feet:	To keep you moving to where you want to go.
Mouth:	To use speech to gain your advantage.
Hands:	To shake to ingratiate yourself with those you need.
Eyes:	To see what you want to see.
Feelings:	To numb so others can't understand them.

Oldster

Arms:	To try to reach out and hug.
Feet:	To try to get you to safety and security.
Mouth:	To speak to anyone who will listen.
Hands:	To touch lovingly anyone who will come close.
Eyes:	To search for loved ones who don't come.
Feelings:	To wear openly for those willing to understand.

Thoughts: Stages of life • Maturity • Change of needs

ALCOHOL (n.) - an intoxicating drink

alcohol

I'm shy. I really don't think I look very good.
  No one is interested in being around me.
I'm bored. I'd like to meet someone,
  but why should I go over to them?
They probably won't like me.
I'm lonely.

"A drink? Sure!" It will give me something to do.
  It tastes good. Maybe, I'll have another.
  It's getting warm in here. I'll loosen my shirt collar.
  Is someone looking at me?
"Hello there! Can I buy you a drink?
  OK, I'll have one too." I have to be sociable.
A couple of drinks will loosen me up.
  I'm funny when I'm relaxed.
A few more drinks just to get a buzz on.
  It's a great feeling. I can go over to anyone I want.
    They'll like me, I know.
  I like to sing and dance.
    So I get a little loud? So what!
      If they don't like it, tough!

"You think you're smart, don't you!
  You better not come near me.
  OK, I'll calm down." They really make me mad!

"Another drink? Sure!" That's what I need!
  Then everything will be OK.
"What was I saying?
  Oh yeah, well, I really want to be with you."

(continued)

"What's your name?
I can tell you really like me.
Let's get out of here and go to my place."

"Whoops, watch where you're going. Jerk!
He bumped into me.
Did you see them jump when I threw the glass?
Money? Sure, I can pay.
I really like you! You think I'm really great?
Yeah, I know. Everyone tells me that.
I love you too!" I feel so good!

* * *

What's that light? Morning already?
Ow, my head. I can't open my eyes.
Coffee! That's what I need.
"Who are you?
Oh, yeah. I guess it's time for you to go home.
Yeah, well, it was really nice meeting you too.
You love me? Oh, yeah, thanks! I'll call you."

This place is a mess. Oh, my head!
Just a little more sleep.
Wow, I must have had some night.
I hope I didn't do anything I shouldn't have.
It's lonely here! I'm so tired, and I hurt.
Where's all my money?

That light hurts! I have such a headache.
Food? I can't even look at it.
I guess I'll be all right at work.
Nobody better give me a hard time,
or I'll really let them have it.

(continued)

Maybe a drink will help me settle my stomach.
Ah! That's better.
I look terrible. No one will ever want to meet me looking like this.

I'm lonely. Maybe tonight I'll go out.
A couple of drinks and I'll feel OK.
I don't need to drink. It's just to be sociable.
It helps me unwind.
I can stop anytime I want to.
I just don't want to . . . .

Thoughts: Alcoholism • Consequences • Social drinking • Out of control

alcohol

ALONE (adj.) - apart from others

alone

Keep out! I don't need you!
  I can handle my own world
    and solve my own problems.

Don't touch me! I will shy away.
Don't give advice!
  I hear you, but I won't listen.

You believe in me? Why?
  I failed at what I've tried.
  I was rejected by those I love.
  I made mistake after mistake.

I will not love and be rejected.
I will not trust and be hurt.
I will not listen and have my hopes smashed.
I will not try and fail again.

Leave me alone! I'm afraid.

I can't reveal myself.
  Then you would see me as I really am,
    understand how I really feel,
    know what I really need and want.

(Please don't stop caring!)

Thoughts: Why push others away? • Need for others • Alone by choice vs. circumstance

☐ ambition

Ambition
is the spark needed
to ignite your engine of potential
propelling you toward your goal.

☐ anger

anger

Anger is an out-of-control imploding fire
wasted on destructive self-pity.
If controlled,
its energy could fuel constructive growth.

Source: See P. 10

As hurt becomes healing,
anger subsides.

ANGER (n.) - a strong feeling of displeasure

anger

Anger is an out-of-control imploding fire
  spontaneously fueled by blazing feelings
    of perceived hurts to our psyche.

Anger rages through our once-at-peace self-image.
  It deafens us to hearing those trying to help
    and blinds us to the reality of what actually is.
  It knocks our equilibrium off balance
    leaving us unable to objectively focus.
  It shuts down our ability to act rationally,
    trapping us in uncontrolled emotional extremes.

To relieve the intolerable pressure building inside,
  we flailingly rush for a way out to get relief
    knocking over any caring others nearby.
We lash out at those closest to us
  because we don't know how to direct
    our discomfort to anyone other than those
      with whom we feel most safe.

As the intense inner-fire gradually subsides,
  embers of resentment still churning within
    may revive deeply hidden past hurts
      that can start our emotions burning again.

To control the destructive fire of feelings inside
  from rekindling, we must clear out the residual
    smoke and ash of past damage.
Only then can the once devastating fire of trapped anger
  be used as energy to fuel constructive growth.

Thoughts: Anger vs. danger • Self-control • Resentment

☐ answers

What good are answers
if there are no questions?

☐ appearance

It's not who you are
but who you think you are
that is most visible.

APPEARANCE (n.) - our looks, persona, public view

appearance

Why do I fix up?
I worry if my hair isn't just so,
if my clothes are up-to-date and fit just right
and if the colors are complementary.

It's not for me. I can't see myself.
But I can see your reaction.
Do you like and accept me?
Do you think I'm attractive?

Appearance tells a lot:
What I think of myself.
Who I want to attract and for what purpose.

I build an image of how I want others to see me.
If you're attracted to the package,
the wrapping, the glitter and the image,
then maybe you'll want to look inside
to see what I'm really like
and get to know me as I really am.

Do I interest you?

Thoughts: Style • Conformity • Self-image

☐appetite

What satiates our appetites
TODAY
becomes our expectation and norm
for TOMORROW.

☐applause

Some seek applause and recognition
for their performance
rather than for the person they could be.

Source: See P. 105

applause

□ appreciate, appreciation

Learn to appreciate
the delicate, moderate, subtle nuances of life
before building up a tolerance for
the strongly spiced and seasoned experiences
that may tempt you along the way.

If you can't have
what you want,
learn to appreciate
what you have.

Appreciation . . .
a seed from which germinate
inspiration,
warmth,
incentives
and hope.

Appreciation
is ego-fuel.

☐art

Art
is from
the heart.

☐attention

Rain makes the woods green
as leaves perk up
after receiving their life-refreshing sustenance
grateful for the shower of attention
in which they were bathed.

Your attention has the power
to push me to stage center
by shining your nourishing spotlight
of interest on me.
Source: P. 182

When we try to impress everyone
who gives us attention,
we are performing as animated marionettes
dependent on others
to give us our cues and control our moves.
We become trapped in the limited spotlight
of others' attention
rather than finding our own light
of independence and self-control.

ATTITUDE (n.) - a feeling reflected in one's appearance or behavior

attitude

If you are weary of the dreary
and tired of being sad or mad,
try exuding a positive attitude
to get rid of feeling bad.

Smile for a little while
and put on a happy face.
Think of the pleasant and upbeat
to help change the pace.
You may not feel less serious
or chase all your blues away,
but if even for an instant,
you'll lighten your load for today.

So lift your spirits with a glint,
a chuckle, tune or wink.
Give yourself a little tickle
and find happy thoughts to think.
It may not last, it may not stay,
but your lighter frame of mind
will be a welcome respite
along the continuum of your time.

Thoughts: Be positive • Think happy • Changing moods

☐ attract

People are like magnets.
What and who they attract
shows the kind of vibes they send out.

B *Pp. 16-20*

☐bad

BAD is harsh and instantaneous.
The results are immediate, destructive
and unforgettable to the recipient.
GOOD is gentle and takes time to understand.
The results are often not recognized
or even fully appreciated until the
recipient is without it.

☐become

To BE
is
to BECOME.

becoming

☐book

A learned friend waiting to share,
hoping to give, asking nothing back except
the opportunity for your attention. Source: P. 18

A book is a bridge
from one who wrote,
wanting to share thoughts and feelings,
to one who reads,
willing to listen and consider new ideas.
Source: See P. 18

BOOK (n.) - a written or printed work bound together

book

A melange of indelicate scratches of ink
indelibly inscribing feelings, ideas and thoughts
on the intangible flow of time.

An enticing package for the curious to open
containing a unique gift for each one it attracts.

A scramble of ideas
blended together into a delectable dish
to be consumed with relish
by an appreciating connoisseur.

A bauble for the illiterate.
A feast for the gourmet.
An instructor for one who wants to know.
An invitation for the novice.
A necessity for one desiring to learn.
A refreshment for the weary.
A sedative for the overcharged.

(continued)

A source of strength for the seeker.
A spark for the uninspired.
A stimulant for the tired.

A learned friend
waiting to share, hoping to give,
asking nothing back except
the opportunity for your attention.

A bridge
from one who wrote,
wanting to share thoughts and feelings,
to one who reads,
willing to listen and consider new ideas.

A labor of love for the producer;
an opportunity to learn for the consumer.

A treasure just waiting to be found
to give of its value.

Thoughts: Learn to read • Read to learn • Libraries

book: A learned friend

☐ bragging

Bragging is truth
 with the volume turned up too loud.

☐ bravado

***Bravado* is often so forceful**
because it is propelled
by a lot of hot air.

☐ bus

Missed the bus in the morning?
WHAT TO DO:
Be angry and vent?
Be patient and wait?
Find another way to get
to where you want to go?
Give up and go back home?
YOUR CHOICE!

bus

BUS (n.) - large motor vehicle with passengers

bus

There are very many problems
for which solutions are hard to find.
Poverty, disease and hunger
have many people in a bind.

Consumption of drugs and alcohol
all lead to much abuse,
and theft and crime and other ills
have no good excuse.

There's litter in the streets I cross
and habitable houses falling down.
Unemployment takes a heavy toll
even with jobs around.

I can't cure pollution
or bring the world to peace.
Political ills and rivalries
have solutions out of my reach.

But one thing that I do know,
and it's as clear as clear can be,
that there are ways to help each other
with things we can plainly see.

So when I'm on the corner
and in a definite rush,
please think of me a little,
and *STEP TO THE BACK OF THE BUS!*

Thoughts: Courtesy • Be considerate of others

C *Pp. 21-43*

☐ **can** (v.)

Those who can, should!

☐ **camouflage** (n.)

Most people really judge us
by how they think we look
instead of getting to know us
by what's inside the *'book.'*
Source: P. 22

CAMOUFLAGE (n.) - disguise to blend in
with the surroundings

Camouflage

I shove healthy well-developed feet
into shoes that are much too small.
I clog my pores with powdered clay
to cover imperfections over all.

I squeeze my extended tummy
by wrapping it all around
and starve myself for days and days
so I don't have to look so round.

My hair is burnt with chemicals
and treated with strong color.
I put fake stuff on lips and cheeks
to brighten up what's really duller.

So after all the pain and work,
what you think you see
is the result of extended efforts
to hide what's really me.

There's nothing wrong with improvement
from healthy natural things,
but it's so much easier to camouflage
even with the artificiality it brings.

Most people really judge us
by how they think we look
instead of getting to know us
by what's inside the *'book.'*

(continued)

So for many, it's not how you feel that counts,
but what you appear to be.
I just have to remember that
so I won't judge others who I see, and also
to be careful not to make that person me!

Thoughts: Have a kind eye • Feel good about yourself

CANDLE (n.) - a wick in wax; lit to produce light

Candle

A candle once lit flickers brightly to life.
It captures rapt attention and glows to its
full potential before it sputters and extinguishes
that which was so special.

For some, their wick burns frantically and flares
to ecstatic heights using up their reserves
too quickly to be remembered or appreciated.
For others, their flame leaps chaotically
and creates such excess that it spreads
a fiery horror of destruction so bad that all
in its path are sorry it ever came into existence.
There are those who to survive and keep going
have to sputter hard to overcome poor construction
and are exhausted from the effort.
They extinguish their flame of potential too quickly
without much chance of making their world
brighter for having been there.

But for most, their candle burns steadily
with a consistent and even flame, glowing
and growing dependably and conservatively
as it uses its finite time to the fullest degree.

Thoughts: Do good when you can • Burn-out

□ can't

Some people live in the world of
"I will!"
because they really believe
"I can't!"

□ caring

Your caring has the power
to exit me out of
my loneliness.
Source: P. 182

Caring hurts
when the taker depletes
the giver's reservoir
of kindness
and leaves only an empty space
that was previously filled
with love.

CENSORED (v.) - suppress selected parts

Censored

How are you?
Censored! No comment!
Personal!
I refuse to divulge!
Mental blocks, Walls,
Barriers in place!
Keep away!
Keep out!
None of your business!
Who cares!
Not important to anyone!
Turned off!
Tuned out! Out of reach!
Drifting in space!
Encapsulated! Isolated!
Do not approach!
Do not encroach! Do not ask!
I won't tell!
The End!

Thoughts: Isolation vs. openness • Willing to trust

censored: Keep out

CHANCE **(n.) - an opportunity to do or achieve something**

Chance

Here I sit!
Bursting with energy.
Burdened with time.
Having abilities, qualities and skills,
but I can't get the chance
to put them to use.

So where do I go from here?
Every door seems closed.
I spin my wheels trying,
but I don't get anywhere.

I want so much to amount to something.
I need someone to help me
open a door just a little,
hear about an opportunity or
know where to go and what to do.
I need the chance to
rekindle my hopes,
refresh my dreams and
find my way.
I'll do the rest.

HELP WANTED! PLEASE!

Thoughts: Find opportunities • Network • Help others • Be prepared

☐ **change** (v.)

Change
is a constant!

Change starts with WILLPOWER.

Willpower becomes HABIT.

Habit becomes CHANGE.

CHANGE (v.) - become something different

Change

When we stand in the same spot too long,
we gradually sink into a hole
of our own making.
Our environment encloses and traps us
inside the wall of our familiar.

Here we comfortably exist,
unwilling to climb out,
fearing what we cannot see
that is outside of our chosen niche.

To free ourselves
requires us to leave what we know
and move toward that which
we do not know.

Change is a scary journey
from what we are used to
and toward what we hope will be.

Thoughts: Habits • Try new things • Grow & Learn

□ character

Having character
is saying *"NO!"*
to those things that can HURT us,
no matter how available, attractive or popular
they may appear to be;
and saying *"YES!"*
to those things that can HELP us,
no matter how remote, unattractive or difficult
they may appear to be.

CHASE (v.) - pursue in order to catch

Chase

I chase rainbows. They are so pretty!
I wonder what I would do
if I actually caught one.

I chase the sun,
but it leaves me every night!
I chase the wind,
but it doesn't let me catch it.

Still I try and try
as if failure only increases my desire.
Perhaps I chase intangibles
because I really just need a purpose
not the end result.

Thoughts: Enjoy what you do • Have fun • Dream

CHILD (n.) - youth below the age of
full physical development

Child

The child:
Not automated by impersonal treatment.
Not folded, spindled or mutilated by bad habits.
Not polluted by unkindness, processed by hurts,
contaminated by hatred nor transistorized by rejection.

The child growing with layers added to:
Cover sensitivities, deaden pain and hide spontaneity.
Restrain affection and limit flexibility, hope and desires.

The child maturing is made up to:
Exude confidence and exhibit knowledge.
Show strength and mask emotions.
Cement in the cracks, flaws and defects of maturity.
The child still inside: Believing! Hoping!
Waiting for someone to provide love, give support
and offer strength and security!

The child grown and living in a self-made future:
Designed by imagination, chance and hope.
Sewn up by experiences and deeds.
Tailored from the pattern of early
efforts, successes, failures, errors and trials.
Worn as a finished product;
complementary if carefully designed,
showing faults of workmanship where not corrected.

One looking back on childhood
and wondering where the future went.

Thoughts: Childhood • Maturation • Choices & chances

□ children

Children

are the world's Spring.

Source: P. 31

CHILDREN **(n.) - young persons below the age of full physical development**

Children

Children have the power of unconditional love.
They know, show and act on who they like.

Children have the power of wonder.
They hear with quick reactions
and respond immediately without fear.
They look with unquenchable interest.
They touch with incredible awe.
They soak up all learning that comes their way.

Children have the power to resist hurt
and can change course, goals and interests quickly.
They disbelieve pain and cruelty and take chances.

Children are oriented toward goals and successes.
They are willing to try endlessly.
They rebound, move on fearlessly and try again.
They do not understand defeat or limits.

Children have the power to signal feelings.
They reach out for attention.
They show hurt, pain, loneliness and need.
They effuse pleasure, warmth and caring.

Children can believe in magic and wonder.
They can be distracted away from
boredom, hurt and unhappiness.

(continued)

Children have the power to hold on to time.
They cherish the moment and love the immediate.
They totally absorb the now
until a new distraction pulls.

Children have the ability to bring joy.
They make us smile.
They open our eyes to wonder and the new.
They give us hope for a new tomorrow.

Children are the world's Spring.

Thoughts: Sensitivity • Protection • Teachable moments

☐ choices

We may not be in control
of our opportunities,
but we are in control of our choices.

Make discriminating choices
from your menu of opportunities.

We don't always have solutions;
sometimes we only have choices.

Choices
are the rungs of life's ladder
and lead us to where we end up.

**The future awaits
whatever choices we make today.**

☐ circles

Some move aimlessly and directionless
  in the same familiar circles.
But they do so with determination and speed
  in the hope that new paths
    will magically appear.

☐ circumstances

It's not your circumstances,
  but what you make of them that matters.

☐ civilization

Civilization
in its essence
is reliance on the word.

civilization

COLD (adj.) - unfriendly, indifferent, unfeeling

Cold

A cold world exists for many whose icy exteriors
  conceal the fears, hopes and good qualities frozen inside,
    perhaps preserving them for some future use.

Warmth emanates from some others
  who travel through their world
    caring away fears, pain and hurts, and
      smiling away loneliness, tears and self-doubts.
  They melt away the icy exteriors of those they meet.
    Their inner flame of kindness flickers brightly
      as it reaches out for the inner good of others.

For some, the flame of friendliness extended to them
  may only melt their frosted outer shell of fears
    dampening others' attempts to reach
      the inner glow trapped inside.
The world then remains cold to them as they
  block out beauty, discourage warmth and caring,
    freeze out pleasantness and ignore sparks of kindness.

Spread the fires of kindness
  with a smile, kind words, nice deeds, courtesy,
    a helping hand and belief in and trust of others.
Accepting the flame of compassion makes it glow brighter.
  Feeding warmth will intensify it.

Kindle the buried flame of kindness in others
  by igniting your own spark
    and warming the world around you.

Thoughts: Don't freeze others out • A warm personality

□comfortable

When you are comfortable with yourself
then you may be willing to try
at what is uncomfortable.

COMFORT-ZONE (n.) - a situation where
one feels safe or at ease

Comfort-zone

Standing in the soft comfort-zone
of our expected familiar,
we contentedly sink into its secure stillness.
Ultimately we grow roots that bind us in the place
where our stationary horizon allows us to be.

When our universe suddenly shoves us out of
our complacent spot, we unexpectedly bump into
an unfamiliar and confusing terrain.
Uncomfortably out of the security of our familiar,
we longingly look back at what was
and anguish over why things could not
have remained as they were.

Feeling vulnerable, lost and confused
by the fearful new void, we find ourselves
exposed to a new horizon
not previously seen or considered.
It stretches our vision beyond the comforting zone
In which we had grown so attached.
If our attention stays overwhelmingly focused
on the loss of the familiar, we will be unable
to see beyond that guarded spot
in which we were so entrenched.

(continued)

When we are ready to take that first step
toward accepting our new reality,
new paths will welcomely open to us,
and we can look ahead with glimmers
of anticipation at new possibilities.

Abrupt change, so difficult to accept,
can become a challenging opportunity for us
to use familiar experiences of the past
as a base to explore new options.

The empty void of our lost familiar
can then become a comforting cushion
for the new opportunities that await us.

*Thoughts: Don't fear change • Learn from the past •
Challenge yourself • Take opportunities*

comfort zone

COMMON-SENSE **(n.) - good sense and judgment**

Common-sense

Common sense and practical things
take time and careful thought.
The fads, the ads, the faster things
do not usually pay off.

The body has its needs,
and to maintain it takes much care.
To destroy and hurt for effect and show
never gets us anywhere.

A little time spent in planning
and thoughtful consideration
can make a major difference in
our future situation.

So think of today as just a step away
from the results that appear tomorrow.
Then some care today can insure against
some in-the-future sorrow.

Thoughts: Plan • Take care of you • Be practical

□ compete

Honorable folks just can't compete
when a few others change rules at will.
Keeping pace with nasties then
becomes a very bitter pill.

Source: P. 160

☐ complain

We often complain about what is
because we don't realize what isn't.

COMPLAIN (v.) - express dissatisfaction

Complain

Some find it so easy to complain.
They just shout out what's on their mind.
It's preferable that we restrain our words
to the more reasonable kind.

Sometimes releasing anger
at perceived hurts is what you seek.
But be careful that you realize
you can hurt others when you speak.

Loudness does not increase the accuracy of words.
Remember intolerable pain can be caused
by hurtful things that are heard.

Those who must receive complaints
should always consider the source.
The most important thing that they can do
is to not make matters worse.

The softest voice should always be
eagerly sought after and found.
It's important to help everyone work together
to find some common ground.

You can always fuss to your heart's content,
but do so with reflection.
Remember your main purpose is to get
a positive and productive reception.

So stop, look and listen when others share concerns.
Then work together as best you can
so good results can be earned.

Thoughts: Words affect others • Listen • Be nice

□ compliments

Compliments are like honey.
To some, they are sweet
creating a lingering desire to taste them again.
To others, they create a sticky residue
that feels uncomfortable, undesirable and unwanted.

□ contact

Contact with another
completes the circuit between giver and taker
allowing the current of acceptance to flow,
lighting up both worlds
and making each feel needed and wanted.

Source: See P. 132

CONTRADICTION (n.) - opposite statements or ideas

Contradiction

The adult living as the child:
Craves attention from the uncaring
but ignores those who care.
Dreams fantasy
but lives nightmares.
Lights up a stage
but lives in shadows.
Runs after what is wanted
but not what is needed.
Works hard
to get the negative.

Or is that the child
unwilling to mature and become an adult?

Thoughts: Face reality • Grow up

☐ cope

We are often experts at escape
but apprentices at coping.

☐ could

**If you don't do what you COULD,
then what might be,
WON'T.**

**Fewer *"I could's"*
make for more
*"I will's."***

Those who say
"I could"
probably can't.

☐ courage

courage

COURAGE (n.) - brave, daring, bold

Courage

How courageous you must feel!
Deceiving others. Telling expertly crafted lies.
Using just the right words to get what you want.
Now discovered, you must run from those
who trusted, believed in and cared about you.

Did you show courage?
Or was it all a masquerade to cover your fear of:
Telling truth but not being believed?
Caring but being rejected?
Trusting but being deceived?
Trying but experiencing failure?

It took courage to survive your past –
the pain, hurts and disappointments.
Now, you can learn to use your courage to:
Accept those who offer friendship.
Do good.
Face responsibilities.
Trust and believe in others.
Try even if it means not always succeeding.
Value truth and integrity.

Then you will develop the strength to
have pride and confidence in yourself
and allow others to believe in,
have pride in and trust you.

Thoughts: Deal with problems • Search for solutions • Fight obstacles

COURTESY (n.) - being polite, considerate, respectful

Courtesy

When you remember to say *"I'm sorry"*
  for things you forgot to do,
and always say *"Excuse me"* and *"Thank you,"*
  it will make a bit nicer you.
Remember, these little phrases,
  so very easy to say,
can turn a difficult time for others
  into a better day.

But if you don't remember
  to show courtesy and care,
others may think seriously about
  if they really want you there.

Kind words and gracious thoughts
  may seem insignificant and small.
Showing you respect others' feelings
  will keep your character tall.

So build your reputation carefully
  with kind words and deeds you do,
and your courteous actions
  will help others think well of you.

Thoughts: What is courtesy? • Show respect • Why be courteous?

CRAZY (adj.) - not normal; bizarre, weird

Crazy

I LIVE IN A WORLD:

Where crazy is normal.
Bad is good.
Good is naive.
Loud is valid.
Quiet is ignored.

Where lies are truth.
Truth is what you wish.
Facts are false.
Rumor is real.

Where friends are acquaintances.
Acquaintances are friends.
Mean is nice.
Cruel is the norm.

Where crowds create loneliness.
Stimulants bring passivity.
Kindness is suspect.
Integrity is ignored.

Where smart is dumb.
Dumb is listened to.
Gay is sad.
Cool is hot.

Where unnatural is real.
Real is disguised.
Honesty is self-serving.
Grotesque is attractive.

Where passive is active.
Highs make lows.
Rude is strong.
Strong is weak.

(continued)

Where giving is suspect.
Selfish is in.
Caring is unappreciated.
Expecting is expected.

I CAN'T COPE!

Thoughts: Values • What is normal? • Popular influences

☐crutch

When you use a crutch,
realize you have a handicap.

D

Pp. 43-65

☐damage, damaged

Damage corrected
is not the same
as damage not done.

Damage stays real
until we find a way to make it heal.

If something is damaged, we have choices:
FIX it! TOLERATE it! TOSS it!
or STARE at it until you get tired.

Damage is so easy to do
and takes such little effort and thought;
but the results can be devastating,
and repair never brings back exactly what was.

DAMAGED (adj.) - not original condition

damaged

Provided for, controlled, tolerated.
An unwanted child!

Put down, abused, left alone, neglected.
An unhappy youth!

Unrestricted, unsupervised, ignored, left out.
A drifting young adult!

Uncaring, unfeeling, insensitive, aimless.
A damaged adult!

Thoughts: Childhood experiences • Parenting • Self-image

☐ **date**

date

DATE (n.) - social appointment with someone

date

Got a heavy date tonight!
  I feel really good about it.
Got to get ready!
  I'll wear my new jeans. They're just tight enough.
  Hope my hair will look okay;
    I used that new special smelling shampoo.
I want to look my best! Look great! Just right!
  I want everything to be perfect.

We really hit it off!
  When we're together, nothing else matters.
  We like, need and understand each other.
It's nice to have someone special to be with,
  get close to, touch and hold.

I've needed someone to care about me.
  Someone who likes me and has time for me.
  Someone who wants me close.
  Someone to kiss away my tears and hug away my fears.
  Someone to accept me as I am
    and tell me everything is all right.

I wish you had thought about what you were doing
  when you were my age.
Do you realize how hard it has been for me
  knowing you don't care for each other?
I never felt wanted. I always felt neglected and left out.

I was a mistake. The result of a careless moment,
  a quick union, a fit of love.

(continued)

You really didn't want me.
  You weren't ready to have a child.
  I caused you hardship just by being around.
I needed attention, caring and time,
  but you were too busy growing up yourselves.
    When I cried, you got angry.
    When I wanted to hug you, you were too tired.
    When I wanted to talk, you told me to be quiet.
    And when I withdrew, you didn't even notice.

I waited to see you, but you rarely were there.
  I needed company, but you left me alone.
  I needed love, but you gave me money.
  I needed guidance, but you gave me punishment.
Didn't you realize that I was a person too;
  that you couldn't just push me aside as if
    I didn't exist and not expect me to feel it?

I do exist! I had to find my way by myself;
  to hold the hurts inside until I thought I'd burst;
  to look for others to care and give me love.

Well, now I'm the age you were!
  I know what it's like to be unwanted.
You were old enough to create me,
  but you weren't mature enough to be parents.
I sure won't bring a child into this world as you did.

Well, that's in the past. I need love, and I'll find it!
  My date is special! We really get it together.
  This is the real thing.
  Two of us like one - caring, sharing, loving.

(continued)

Tonight we'll make love! Go all the way!
We'll have fun; have a good time together.
Really make it happen.

Don't wait up for me!

Thoughts: Purpose of dating • Results of intimacy • Planning • Sex education • Parenting

□dead-end

When you get to a dead-end,
you can either
stay there and complain
to anyone passing by
or ask someone for directions out.

dead-end

DEATH (n.) - the end of life

death

Hello! Are you waiting for me?
I hurt! I fail! I hate myself!
I bring pain to others! No one cares!

Will I like you? Could I meet you now?
No one will miss me. They won't care.
Will I be better off after we meet?
Free of the pain, hurt, frustrations and failure?

I wish you would come and get me
so I can leave my problems behind.
Will you make my problems go away,
or will they come with me?

Will I remember the good things I've done,
or things I didn't have the courage to face?
Will I regret not using my time more wisely?
Will I be angry at feeling so sorry for myself
when all I had to do was look around
to appreciate what I had?

When I am with you, will I hurt more?
Will I have a better view of how
I could have handled those things
that gave me so much pain?

Will I realize what I could have done to:
Deal with my problems? Do more for others?
Learn more from my experiences?
Appreciate the good things I had?

Perhaps I'll see that it wasn't so bad after all!
But then it will be too late!
You won't let me go back, will you?

In fact, are you really there,
or are you just in my imagination?

(continued)

Perhaps you don't really exist.
Perhaps you are nothingness, blank, a void.
Maybe I'll wait awhile!
Catch you later! I have things to do, NOW!

Thoughts: Solve problems • Get help • Sympathy-getting

☐ deed

A good deed has the power to:
Build up the most damaged of egos.
Erase the deepest emotional scars.
Warm the coldest moods.

☐ dessert

I'm watching my weight. Not sure what to take.
I REALLY LIKE THE CAKE!
After thinking it over, maybe instead
IT WOULD BE BETTER TO HAVE THE BREAD!
But I really care about what I should eat there, so
I'M GOING TO CHOOSE THE PEAR!

☐ destination

Some purposely take paths filled with
DARKNESS, DETOURS, OBSTACLES and POTHOLES
so they don't have to reach their declared destination.

☐ destroy

So easy to destroy!
So hard to mend!

☐ did

'I did' and *'I will'* are both based on desire.
One is fulfilled and the other in the dream-stage still.

DIGNITY (n.) - graciousness, self-respect

dignity

Dignity lost brings some who feel
detached, insignificant and unimportant
to choose and accept a garbage heap as
a comfortable nook for blending into the world.
There, exiled from dignity, they find a rock bottom
on which to lay and decompose attracting
the flies and maggots of despair and ruination.

To exit that darkness requires the desire to change
and a willingness to hope for a better existence.
The ladder up – one rung at a time –
leads into a new and unfamiliar wilderness of choice
where the sunlight of reality reveals a path
to the fresh air of self-caring
and the challenge of possibility.

Each step up is an adventure in survival.
The climb is difficult, the baggage is heavy and
goals are shrouded in clouds of chance and hope.
Each step builds strength in the tired limbs,
the defeated spirit and the damaged self-image
that kept them stuck at rock-bottom.

As each new plateau is reached,
there is a strengthening of resolve and character
that builds confidence to go on
and breaks the chains of pain
so long accepted as one's lot in life.

Thoughts: Change and growth • Action • Self-respect

dignity: Lost

☐ direction

Others can point out a direction,
but we must go on our own.

Direction is a choice.

☐ disadvantages

Use your disadvantages
to your advantage.

☐ disappointment

Disappointment occurs when expectations exceed reality.

DIVING (v.) - jumping into deep water;
- plunge head first

diving

Wow! That diving board looks exciting!
It's very high though.
Don't the divers look great?
So sleek, so athletic, so graceful.
Everybody admires them. They're very popular.

Diving looks so easy.
You just jump off, and the water stops you.
I guess you hold your hands a certain way?
The loops and flips seem difficult.
That must take some practice.

"You're all going to dive?
I've never done it before. Yes, it does look easy."
I'll bet it feels good just free-falling like that.
I don't know if I should do it though.
There must be more to know than just jumping off.

"How do I know I won't like it if I never tried it?
No! No one got hurt today! NO! I'm not chicken!
I'm not afraid to try. I just don't feel like it.
Everybody else is going to do it?
I'll be the only one not trying it?"
Hum! I'll really stand out as different, won't I?

Well, maybe I could try it once. There's always a first time!
I might be excellent and look great.
Then everyone will tell me how good I was.
Well, it seems easy enough!
Just climb up, walk out and jump off. Okay!

(continued)

I'm climbing up, but I still have a long way to go.
  I don't believe how high it looks from up here.
Why do I feel so nervous?

Now I'm at the top. Where's everybody?
  I'm all alone up here. Everyone's looking at me.
    They all seem so far away. They look so little.
I can't stop now. I can't go back down.
  Everyone will laugh at me!

It's hard to keep my balance. The board is so narrow!
  The water seems so far away. I might miss!
Is this the way they hold their hands?

Why am I doing this? What am I doing up here?
  I wish I hadn't said I would.
  I could have made an excuse!
  I could have said *"No!"*
I know my parents would flip if they saw me now.
  Well, they won't know. I won't tell them!

Okay, let's get this over with!
  I don't want to be different or stand out.
  I want everyone to like me.
  I want to be one of the group.

Here I go!
  I can't! I'm scared! I'm all alone! Nobody's here!
    Please help me, someone!
    Please, I don't want to get hurt!
    I won't ever do it again!
    Just let me get through this!
    I don't want to be embarrassed!
Up I go! - - - I'm falling . . . .

(continued)

Where am I? What's going on?
Why are these tubes in me? What happened?
Oh! I hurt so bad! It's hard to see?
Where is everybody?
"Nurse, will I be all right?
Mom, is that you? Why are you crying?
What happened? What did I do?
The dive? Oh!"

Why did I do it? I wish I hadn't!
Why didn't someone stop me?
Why can't I move my legs?
I hurt! Please tell me what's wrong.
Where are all my friends now?

Why didn't I just say *"NO?"*

Thoughts: Peer pressure • It's okay to say "No!" • Feeling embarrassed • Consider consequences

diving: Should I?

☐ do

You are
what you do!

DO what you can, where you are, with what you have
and be confident you have done your best:

To PUSH	*the immovable*	*is futile.*
To PULL	*the recalcitrant*	*is arduous.*
To LIFT	*the massive*	*is troublesome.*
To IMPEDE	*the determined*	*is risky.*
To CONVINCE	*the obstinate*	*is obstructive.*
To DOUBT	*the inevitable*	*is whimsy.*

DO (v.) - make something happen

do

Buy for me,
and I'll learn to want more.
Do for me,
and I'll never learn to do for myself.
Give to me,
and I'll learn to take.
Guard me from criticism,
and I'll expect praise and approval.
Protect me,
and I'll never learn to deal with difficulty.
Run interference for me,
and I'll never learn to find my own way.
Speak for me,
and I'll never learn to speak for myself.
Take me,
and I'll never learn how to go on my own.
Wait on me,
and I'll learn to expect service.
But let me do for myself,
and I'll learn how to survive.

Thoughts: Learn from mistakes • Independence

□door, doors

When you walk me to the door
  and graciously wait there until I go,
it shows you really care a lot,
  and I appreciate it so.

When you keep closing doors behind you,
you may find them locked
if you want to return.

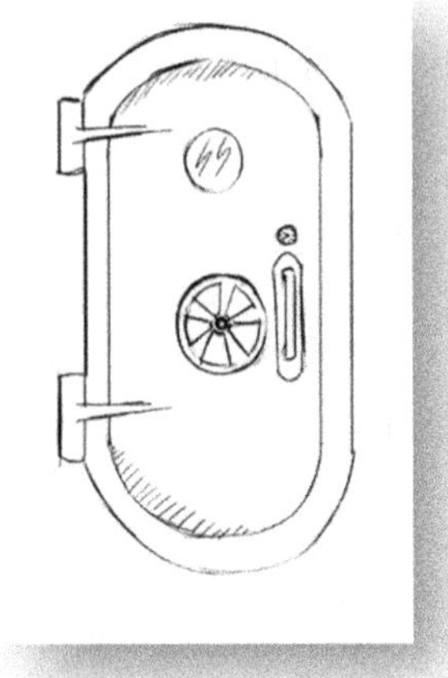

doors: Closed

DREAM (v.) - have images in your mind during sleep
DREAMS (n.) - the images in your mind during sleep

dream (v.)

Dream of sunshine and rainbows
with colors all aglow.

Dream of jet planes, and starships
and places to go.

Dream of candy, and birthdays
and flowers in spring.

Dream of mud pies, and baseball
and every happy thing!

Dream of someone who loves you,
of playing in the park.

Let your dreams be of circus
and sunsets before dark.

Dream of presents, and puppies
and Christmas and snow.

And may all your fondest dreams come true!

song

☐ **dreams** (n.)

Dreams
can fog our vision of ourselves
if too low,
and cloud our view of reality
if too thick.

Source: See P. 59

To reach our dreams,
we must awaken.

Source: P. 59

Dreams
are partially saturated with fairy dust
that aesthetically filters out reality,
clouds the psyche and cushions
the hard knocks of probability.

dreams

***DREAMS* (n.) - images in your mind during sleep**

dreams

Invisible, intangible sensations:
Enthusing hopes.
Exhausting alternatives.
Expanding reality.
Exploring emotions.
Exuding pleasures.
(continued)

Dreams are clouds of euphoric thoughts
high above where we must reach for them.
They extend our vision into pleasurable
surroundings and circumstances.
They leap us over the obstacles
in the *here and now*.
They lift us out of our daily burdens,
problems and troubles.
They can push us out of the present
and paint over the ugliness of reality.
They help us look upwards toward possibilities
not downward at impediments.

Dreams will not come true by themselves.
They give us hope, encouragement, excitement,
goals and a plausible promise of things
we want to come true.

Dreams are not reality.
They can fog our vision of ourselves if too low,
and cloud our view of reality if too thick.

We must work toward our goals:
Examine the obstacles. Plan to overcome.

To reach our dreams,
we must AWAKEN!

Thoughts: Dreams vs. reality •
Making dreams come true

DRINK (v.) - swallow an alcoholic beverage
DRINK (n.) - an alcoholic beverage

drink

Warm. Strong. Friendly. Easy going down.

Slowing movements. Slurring speech.
Dulling perceptions.
Creating cathartic conversations.
Deterring determined deeds.
Evoking enthusiastic espousals.
Making mumbling mutterings.
Slobbering salivary secretions.
Fumbling, bumbling, stumbling, humbling.
Losing, musing, amusing, confusing.
Losing control that you want to hold on to
  and deal with to help solve the problems you
    didn't know what to do about them.

Blurring surroundings. Confusing conversations.
  Noticing nobody. Seeing searing scenes.
Dizzying heights. Devastating depths.
  Unconscionable grumblings
    slurred from slobbering sloths.
Dimming dimensions dropped from distant perceptions.
  Weaving ***Waving*** ***Waiting***
    Worried ***Wasted***
      d
        r
          u
            n
              k !

Thoughts: Effects of alcohol • Social vs. problem drinking

drink

□ drugs

Drugs are magical potions
metamorphosing beauty to monstrous
as seeds of intense self-destruction
are planted in the will of bedazzled seekers
of this deceptive horror.

Source: See P. 62

Drug use is a masquerade
of self-hatred disguised as pleasure
as one runs to get nowhere,
endures pain to suffer, seeks help to hurt
and risks everything to gain nothing.

Source: See P. 63

Drugs that cause the highest highs
make life hit its lowest lows.

Drugs:
Once you use,
you abuse!

DRUGS (n.) - habit forming substances;
- narcotics; thought & behavior altering

drugs

Magical potions
metamorphosing beauty to monstrous
as seeds of intense self-destruction
are planted in the will of bedazzled seekers
of this deceptive horror.

Once caught by the waiting grabbing hook,
unsuspecting independents
become committed beggars
snared in an unrelenting self-assault
on what is left of the once-free person
now stooping to fathomless levels
never believed possible.

The willing victim is trapped as a casualty
of that first insane instant of self-induced horror
that brings false feelings, empty power
and camouflages sadness.

Too late for regrets!
There is no escape, pardon or release
from the prison of mind and spirit.

(continued)

The destructive implosion creates a power surge
  of ruinous exhilarations stabbed into
    a defeated body too tired to resist.
It shatters instincts of self-preservation
  and floods an overburdened brain
    struggling to keep a delicate balance
      between rationality and self-destruction.

Insignificant moments of surrealistic highs
  and quick orgasmic pleasures
    deplete the reservoir of rational actions,
    destroy dreams of what could be,
    push endurance beyond intended limits
      and leave painful scars of devastation
        all too easily ignored or forgotten.

It's a masquerade of self-hatred disguised as pleasure
  as one runs to get nowhere, endures pain to suffer,
    seeks help to hurt, risks everything to gain nothing.

The overburdening power surge
  engulfs and drowns any residual control,
    dreams, emotions or thoughts
  as poisonous dust chokes the very essence
    from the tortured body, only then releasing its victim
      to the rubble of choice in which it wallows.

The new grindstone of habit
  sparks the basest levels of character as
    illusion becomes reality, irrationality becomes logic,
    pain is considered pleasure, caution is unthinkable
      and limits become starting points.

(continued)

Kept company by others
suckered into the same pitiful existence,
each pays the long-term price
for that momentary release from the ordinary.

Devastated by the fallout are those left behind
who once hoped and believed change was possible.
They sadly watch the self-inflicted implosion
of the grotesque quarterback
maneuvering his prized poison
through the gauntlet of caring blockers,
and using every deceitful tactic to avoid being stopped
from completing his destructive mission.

Left with a legacy of emptiness
where specialness once stood,
those who care have unforgiving pain
embedded in tear-stained faces,
indelibly changing love to hate,
pain to pity and disgust and hope
to resigned defeat.

But if some breath and life remain inside
the self-mutilated body and exhausted spirit,
there may still be a chance for the ravaged victim
to rescue himself from the grindstone
of hopelessness.

It requires reviving the will to fight for self-control
and rekindling the spark of appreciation
for an ordinary life filled with the beauty of hope
and the wonder of potential and change.

Thoughts: Being hooked • Effects on loved ones • Health

drugs: Hooked

E *Pp. 65-71*

□ education

Education:
A unique tapestry
woven from threads of past ideas and facts
into our own creative patterns and
displayed in our actions, words and thoughts.

Source: P. 66

We educate
when we open the mind's windows
to the fresh currents
of new ideas and thoughts.

EDUCATION (n.) - giving knowledge

education

An idea discussed. A book used.
A chance to constructively doubt.
Understanding, not just accepting.

A unique tapestry
woven from threads of past ideas and facts
into our own creative patterns
and displayed in our actions, words and thoughts.

A blend of ideas
thickened with facts,
spiced with doubts,
sweetened with interests
and salted with practicality.

Baked in the heat of discussion,
testing and experience,
it is served with assurance
to those who have cultivated a taste
for accepting new thoughts.

Thoughts: Influence of education • Joy of learning

☐ effort

It doesn't take any more effort or energy
to contemplate success
than to expect failure;
to deal with fear
than to run from it;
to do
than to wish;
to listen to good advice
than to be closed to new ideas;
to look ahead
than to look backwards;
to plan
than to worry;
to relive pleasure
than to rehash pain;
to go forward toward a goal
than backwards toward the past.

Source: See P. 74

ENCOUNTER (n.) - an unexpected occurrence

encounter

I stand in the water facing the shore.
The sun shines reflecting sparks of brightness
in all directions from the calm beneath.

As I stand in my chosen spot,
small whitecaps ripple past
creating slight rhythmic motions as they
gently push, pull and lick at my footing.
They bring a feeling of peace and contentment.

(continued)

Suddenly a wave forms and surges toward me.
Its swirling water churns around me
as it heads toward shore.
Its flow encourages me to move
with its graceful but determined push.
I stand firm, resisting its impact,
not heeding the impulse to go with it.

Suddenly it loses momentum, dissipates
and disappears at the shore line.
The water, just moments before
rushing briskly toward shore,
retreats as if the plug
has suddenly been pulled.

Back it comes
pulling with it all that will follow!
Again, I stand firm,
feet dug in by the rushing water
tugging firmly on the sand below me.

As the wave recedes into the mainstream,
I sink into the softness created
as if to announce *"I won't go with you!"*

The impetus and momentum to move ignored,
I remain where I was, at rest,
undaunted with my encounter to change.

*Thoughts: Resisting change • Stubborn •
Determined • Go with the flow*

EULOGY (n.) - speech praising a person at a funeral

eulogy

Do you hear what is being said about me?
  I was nice, kind, good and decent.
I had so much going for me:
  Always helpful. Successful at many things.
  Attractive, intelligent, pleasant. A friend.
  One who loved and cared about others.
  One who wanted love and caring from others.

I was needed, wanted, cared about and loved.
  I meant something to others –
    my smile, words and accomplishments.
What potential I had that was not fulfilled.
  How much I could have given to others
    who had only to accept.
  What pleasure I could have brought
    to those who must now find it elsewhere.
But now that I'm not around, I'll be missed!

I'll be in your memory –
  to remember things we could have done but didn't;
  to be apologized to for all that wasn't done;
  to be missed, wanted and needed;
  to be talked to about things you always wanted
    to say but couldn't or wouldn't;
  to be thought about from time to time.

I can't receive any more hurts or feel the pain
  of rejection, loss or the daily battles to survive.
Thank you for coming and caring!
  I appreciate your words and thoughts.
Farewell forever!

(P.S. Where were you when I needed you?)

Thoughts: Too late • Do when you can • Feeling sorry

□ expect, expectations

Expect the Unexpected!

If you treat me like dirt
TODAY,
don't expect flowers to grow
TOMORROW.

When expectations are too high,
very little will please us
or be appreciated.
When expectations are too low,
anything that comes our way
will be accepted
whether in our best interest or not.

expectations: Waiting

□ experience

The grease of experience
helps us work our way through
the intricate machinery of life.

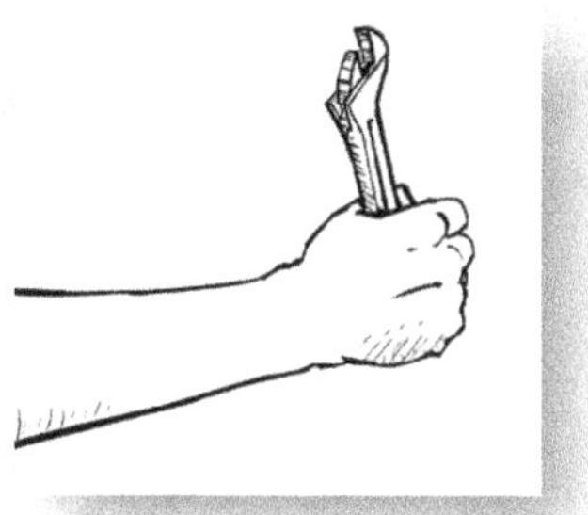

experience

The hard knocks
of experience
chisel the masterpiece
of maturity.

Since we comprehend
only to the limits of our experience,
how important then is it to know
Beauty,
Kindness,
Love
and Warmth?

□ facts

You don't change facts
by denying them.

facts: Denial

□ failure

A failure
is not one who fails,
but one who stops trying.

Some look at failure as success
as long as things don't get worse.

**Some people are expert
at snatching failure out of success.**

Through failure,
we either learn how
to achieve and overcome,
or we are beaten down
into submission and defeat.

FAILURE (n.) - lack of success at what one tries

failure

Feeling sorry for yourself, aren't you?
You were rejected! People hurt you.
You did not succeed at what your tried.
Well, too bad!
What makes you think everything has to go your way?

Do you enjoy reliving pain and frustration?
Do you enjoy showing those who tried to hurt you
that they have succeeded?
That you are a failure?
That you won't amount to anything?

Do you think you'll get even by showing them
what a mess they made of you?
They'll be sorry! That will teach them!
That will serve them right!

Ha! So where does that leave you?

(continued)

Pull out the daggers others left there!
  Let the blood of past hurts flow. It will stop.
Sure, a small scar may be left,
  but then you can stop showing everyone
    the wounds to prove your lack of progress.

How much better it would be to show those
  who let your down, who didn't believe in you,
  who didn't give you a chance
    that you CAN succeed in spite of them.

Concentrate on what caused you to fail
  not on your failures.
Cultivate those who can help you grow
  and avoid those who will drag you down.
Look to what you must do to make success happen.
  Try! Believe! Want! Work at it each day!

It doesn't take any more effort or energy to:
  Contemplate success than to expect failure.
  Deal with fear than to run from it.
  Do than to wish. Plan than to worry.
  Listen to good advice than to be closed to new ideas.
  Look ahead than to look backwards.
  Relive pleasure than to rehash pain.
  Go forward toward a goal
    than backwards toward the past.

In time things change, but you must
  make change happen to your advantage.

How much better it is to stop crying
  about what has passed and start smiling
    about what could come!

(continued)

Stop feeling sorry for yourself
and blaming others for your problems
to justify your lack of accomplishment.
It wastes time, wastes effort
and it wastes you.

Poor you!
Poor sad frustrated you! Poor mistreated hurt you!
Poor useless failure you!

Who said progress is easy?
Things don't just happen by magic.
Be tuned into opportunity.
Have preparation and training.
Be optimistic and try.
Then you will be further along the road to success
than if you wait for it to come to you with
no training, no learning and a defeatist attitude.

You cannot demand things always be your way
or command events to your liking.
The world does not turn for you alone.

You can change and control ONLY yourself.
By changing yourself, you can help others
see you differently.
Opportunities may appear,
and good things may happen.
Then maybe you'll finally find yourself
on the road to success.

*Thought: Fear of success • Self-image • Attitude •
Giving up • Failure as a way of life*

□ fairy-tales

Fairy-tales
have happy endings
because those who create them
want them to!

fairy-tales

□ fall

It doesn't take much to fall.
Only one wrong step
and the rest is downhill.

How can I learn to stand
when I've only known how to fall?

Some remain where they fall
and accept it
as where they must be.

□ fantasy

Some dream in fantasy
because they live in nightmares.

FATHER (n.) - male parent

father

I'm always glad to listen when you share
a problem that you're in.
I try my best to help you
by advising you how to win.
But wouldn't it be easier
if when I say *"Don't do it,"*
you dealt with what's troubling you
by listening to me a bit?

I really try to help you deal
with all that you run into.
So why keep doing what you want
and disregarding what I tell you?

(continued)

I'd like to enjoy life
 and have some peace and quiet,
but because you do not plan ahead
 your woes create an endless riot.

Most people learn from their mistakes
 and don't constantly have them repeated.
You seem to keep doing what brings you to
 the same problems left untreated.

What is done is done and gone
 and, yes, consequences followed after,
but if you keep ignoring warning signs,
 you won't be able to avoid disaster.

So if just once or even more
 you want to give me rest,
please listen to my words and realize
 "Fathers sometimes DO know best."

Thoughts: Parents' role • Listen to good advice

father

FEAR (n.) - anxiety from real or possible danger

fear

Fear of change for you is like
  a set of heavy chains
    that keeps you prisoner
      to the immediate and familiar.
  Any thoughts of what could or might be
    bring forth a flood of obstructive illusions.

Your fear of change becomes:
  A mighty wave
    washing out the visible path ahead.
  A padlocked door
    stopping you from trying to enter.
  A sandstorm
    blinding you from seeing
      what is right in front.
  A narrow winding road
    requiring you to brake, hesitate and stop
      rather than move forward at full speed.

The antidote for fear of change
  is belief in yourself and self-confidence.
These will help you take those first tentative steps
  toward positive choices and real opportunity.

Then what you were so fearful of attempting
  becomes insignificant when you look back.

Thoughts: Power of fear • Face your fears • Immobility

☐ feelings

If someone can *'push your buttons,'*
those feelings were
already exposed and there!

Please consider my feelings with
careful comments, sincere smiles
and thoughtful reactions.

Source: P. 115

Feeling sorry for yourself
wastes time,
wastes effort
and it wastes you!

Source: See P. 75

Our feelings:

Assign value to each experience.
Color our view of the world around us.
Influence our decisions and choices.
Frame our perspective for making
the ordinary pleasurable
and the insignificant painful.

☐ finders

Finders who are keepers
don't believe they are thieves.

FLOWER (n.) - a beautiful gift of nature

flower

My flower is so beautiful.
Each time I visit, I am carried out of my cares.
My thoughts explode in harmony
with its colorful aura.
A smile magically appears on my face, and
my flower becomes the center of my universe.
Everything else moves to peripheral vision.

I look forward to seeing my flower every day.
I can't wait to check to make sure it is doing well.
As I approach, I search for a glimpse of it from afar.
When I am away, I think about it and smile
at the warmth and joy that feeling brings.

We have a special relationship.
It is there for me alone, giving me joy.
It beautifies my world and helps me feel special.
It makes me feel happy and content.
And I am here to be of help in every way I can.

One day I noticed my flower was drooping.
I quickly checked to be sure it had what it needed.
I assured it that everything would be okay
and told it how much it meant to me.
I lingered a little, not wanting to leave, and
began to realize just how lost I'd be without it.

The next day, its color was quickly fading,
and its petals were falling off.
I pleaded for it to be just like it had been.
I wanted it to be beautiful, special and
whole again just like it always had been for me.
As I slowly left, I looked back and hoped
that tomorrow it would be okay.

(continued)

When I returned the next day, it was no longer.
  Its color had faded. The bloom was gone.
    It was beginning to disappear
      into its surroundings.
All that was left
  where my beautiful flower had been
    was a dark frightening void that made me
      feel cold, lost, empty and alone.

I still walk by the familiar spot
  where its presence and warmth had once been,
    but my flower is no longer there.
But strangely, as I walk along, I notice other
  things of beauty I hadn't noticed before.

I realize my flower, just by being, had shown me
  how to experience beauty everywhere
    and to feel joy, happiness and peace.
The gifts my flower gave me remain
  as wonderful treasures, the essence of which
    I can revisit again and again.

My flower sprang from the very spot
  that now seems so empty; and it went back
    to the very place from which it came.
My flower is now part of nature's eternal cycle,
  replenishing that from which new life springs.

My flower was my teacher, mentor and guide.
  The special influence my flower left behind
    still touches me deeply and profoundly.
Its lessons remain for me to experience
  and share over and over again.

I feel at peace now. What was once here for me
  gave me what it was supposed to give.
I took what it gave and feel that gift
  is still a part of me.

(continued)

I love my flower and always shall.
I miss the specialness that was ours to share.
But somewhere in the deep recesses of my being,
it still lives, blooms, enriches and
continues to give me its precious gifts.

My flower will always be a part of me.
What I learned from my flower continues
to light my way when the world seems dark
and helps me recognize beauty all along my path.

I owe it to my flower to share the beauty and love
it gave me in such abundance while it was still here.
In that way, my flower will continue
to live on through me
and will always be there for me
as I continue on without it.

(Happy Mother's Day! 1997)

Thoughts: Memories as treasures • Influence • Acceptance

☐ forgiveness

Forgiveness of ourselves and others
is a self-determined tool
that stops the past from overwhelming us.

It pulls us out of the quicksand of wondering.
It releases us from the disabling anger, resentment
and ever-present pain of reliving
difficult past moments and disappointments.

It refocuses our attention on *What Can Be!*
and allows the precious present
to shower us with possibilities and opportunities
for a productive future.

FORTRESS (n.) - heavily protected, closed off

fortress

I built a wall high and strong
  to keep anyone from getting too close.
I activated security alarms to shut off
  the entrances to my psyche.
I dug a moat to foil those
  who might slip by my other defenses.
I use a shell as my personal armor to stop anyone
  from reaching my innermost self.

I sharpened my powers of detection to alert me
  to that which could cause emotional damage
    and to enable me to run and hide at the
      slightest detection of encroachment
        on my feelings of self-worth.

My defenses are also there to protect me
  from reaching out and trusting anyone
    attempting to breech my emotional security.

How difficult it is to always be on guard,
  but negative experiences have left lasting
    emotional scars and have become radar settings
      against hurtful words and insincere actions.

I suspect attempts to get close as potential invasions:
  Kind words trip the alarm.
  Interest and caring close the gates.
  Friendly gestures and overtures are warily seen
    as possible security breaches.

(continued)

And if perchance my need for love and acceptance
does somehow manage to emerge for others to see,
I can activate my protective defenses and
pull back before I become totally compromised.

Loneliness is the price I pay for
being unwilling to trust or to be left vulnerable.
I await a hero to release me
from my self-imposed prison of isolation.

Maybe that hero is already here inside,
and it is self-acceptance and self-love
that are my keys to finally being free.

Thoughts: Trust carefully • Self-image • Hurt feelings

□ friend, friendship

friend

FRIEND (n.) - person you know well and are fond of

friend

I am a friend:
I can be trusted, relied on, believed.
I can be talked to, looked to for help.

I am a friend:
I feel your pain when you hurt.
I share your hopes when you dream.
I show pride when you succeed.

I am your friend:
I believe in and care about you.
I am here when you need me.

P.S. I need a friend, too!
Are you interested?

Thoughts: Be a good friend • Value friendship

□friendship

Friendship:
A cacophonous noise
finding an appreciating ear
to turn it into
a harmonious overture.

Source: See P. 87

One must flee from the
Bonds of friendship
if they ever become
Chains of abuse.

Friendship:
An incredibly strong bond of choice,
yet fragile enough to be shattered
in an instant if trust is broken.

Source: See P.87

FRIENDSHIP (n.) - a relationship between friends

friendship

A cacophonous noise:
Finding an appreciating ear
to turn it into a harmonious overture.

A commitment:
To believe in, care about, compromise and share.

A fragrance:
Intangible, yet bringing warmth and joy.
Delicate, yet pervasive and all encompassing.
Invisible, yet providing sunlight and color
to an otherwise insipid existence.

An exquisite gem: Precious in value.

Nourishment: Enriching growth, meaning and purpose.

A sweet: Luscious and tasty.

An incredibly strong bond of choice:
Yet fragile enough to be shattered in an instant
if trust is broken.

A two-way street:
With plenty of room for individual movement, but
easily blocked if goals get in each other's way.

Thoughts: Building • Maintaining • Accepting

□future

If you keep looking back to your PAST,
you can trip over your PRESENT
and stumble into your FUTURE.

For some, a possible future
is often held prisoner
to a destructive past.

□gem

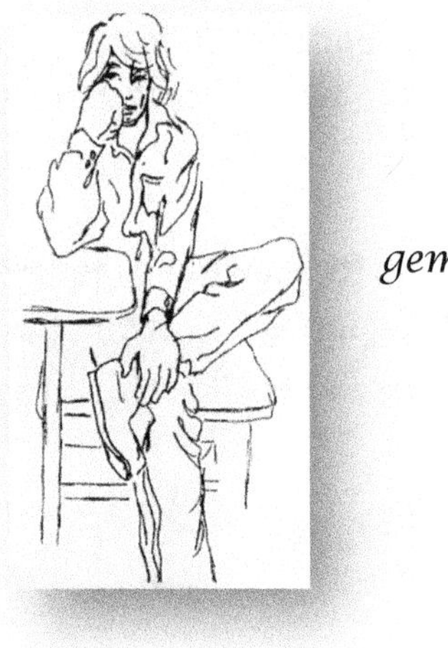

gem

GEM (n.) - a precious stone cut for use as a jewel;
- something very valuable and special

gem

Brilliant, beautiful, priceless.
Coveted, desirable, cared for.
Magnificent in quality.

Shining, sparkling.
Many facets waiting to reflect light
and give joy, pleasure and meaning.

A charismatic presence dazzling.
Adorning and bringing out the best in others.
Changing plainness to sparkle,
shadows to brightness
and emptiness to fulfillment.
Adding purpose and significance
to those whose lives are touched.

But it lies undiscovered.
Dull and unsparkling.
Its gifts hidden. Giving nothing.
Unrecognized. Unrefined. Unfulfilled.

A remnant of nature waiting to be found.
A potential untapped. A treasure unused
just waiting to give of its essence.

Thoughts: Potential • Hidden Value • Undiscovered

□ gift

ACCEPTING a gift
with appreciation and graciousness
is as important as *GIVING* a gift
with kindness and care.

□give, giving

Don't try to give
what you don't have!

GIVE (v.) - freely transfer possession of;
- help by providing something of value

give

Hi! I care about others.
I give from the heart.
I share, offer, provide and extend myself.
I truly want to help!

You came and were in need!
You took, used and accepted everything
and then wanted more.

But now I have given all I have!
I am depleted and empty.
I am now in need!

P.S. Is there someone
who will give to me?

Thoughts: Realistic caring • Being taken advantage of

Some people's idea of giving
is to make themselves able to take.

□go

Wherever we go,
we take ourselves with us.

□goals

Goals must be a little more than *'Reality'* but a little less than *'Hope.'*

□good

One can't do
too much *'Good,'*
or too little *'Bad!'*

Good adds to
rather than
subtracts from the world.

**Always look for the good in others,
not just at how good others look.**

Source: P. 250

Good people
are powerful sources of energy.
They brighten the world
with hope and confidence
for those within the electromagnetic pull
of their nourishing personalities.

**Evil has no bottom.
Good has no top.**

GOOD can never be drowned
in any flood of *BAD*.
It will always float to the surface
when the opportunity is right
and create positive currents
that flow in hopeful directions.
If we go with its flow,
it will encourage us to move with it
until we can move on our own
to buck the tide of *BAD*
that seems to be overwhelming us.

GOOD (n.) - integrity; morally right; beneficial

good

GOOD:

Increases the quality of the world.
It heals, encourages and supports growth.
It brings sunlight to darkness
and hope to despair.

GOOD:

Shows up *BAD*
for what it really is.

Thoughts: Good builds • Bad destroys

GRATEFUL (adj.) - showing appreciation;
- being thankful

grateful

If you like to see the rainbow,
you must put up with some rain.

If you appreciate feeling good,
you probably have experienced some pain.

If you're feeling down or sad or lost,
remember how you've been blessed.

If you're thinking you'd like more than you have,
remember when you made do with less.

If you're grateful for what you have
and what you are able to do,
then you'll be able to better understand
how to appreciate being you.

*Thoughts: Perspective • Appreciation •
Think in positives*

□ grow

grow

☐grow

Some, like unbloomed flowers,
grow in the darkness of rejection and self-doubt.
Faced away from the sunlight
of real caring and attention, they are unable to root
in that which nourishes self-worth
keeping their potential beauty and quality
undeveloped and undiscovered.

See P. 193

GROWTH (n.) - development, maturation;
- physical or emotional

growth

When the seeds for a productive life are planted in
the rocky terrain of limited opportunity and neglect,
their potential remains deeply buried
in that inhospitable soil fostering
bad habits, poor choices and low self-image.

To grow and flower to their fullest potential,
the fragile seedlings need the help of caring others to:
Carefully fertilize them with meaningful attention.
Expose them to the sunlight of opportunities.
Provide protective oversight to guard against
damage from bad influences.
Prune rough spots with encouragement and praise.
Refresh their depleted reservoir of self-esteem and hope.
Weed out obstacles using good suggestions and advice.

(continued)

Will you allow your qualities
to grow, bloom and flower for all to be proud of,
or have detrimental forces so deeply touched you
that growth has already been irreparably stunted?

Has the heat of frustration, the storm of rejection
and the flood of too much giving to you
depleted your desire for proper growth?
Have insensitive others trampling on your self-image
leached you of innate compassion, hope and trust?
Have bad habits so weakened your roots that they are not
strong enough to hold the promise of further growth?

Nourishing love sprinkled by caring others
can bring you hope for new growth
unless you let it drain right through to the
bedrock of self-abuse and lie there unused.

You can choose to do the hard work of growth,
fulfill your potential and grow beyond expectations.
You can reach beyond the weeds clogging your vision
of possibilities and let the sunlight of opportunity
nourish you toward full blooming.

Those who believe in you and want to help
keep hoping for a positive harvest.
Will they be able to experience the pride of your blooming,
or will they be left exhausted from trying to root out
the destructive forces of your poor choices and habits
that quickly resurface once they are out of sight?

Let's wait to see the fruits of their labor!

Thoughts: Work at growth • Be willing to grow • Self-help

GUARDIAN-ANGEL (n.) - spirit believed
to watch over and protect

guardian-angel

A Guardian Angel waiting to serve may not be visible,
but it is just a hope away:
Proactively moving obstacles out of your way.
Protectively watching for your missteps.
Helping you up if you fall.

The relationship is all one-sided.
You need do nothing to get help
or to make the relationship grow,
unlike personal relationships that will grow
only if maintained and nurtured.

Guardian Angels spend their time on those
who are not yet ready to help themselves, or who
don't yet understand that choices have consequences.

The Guardian Angel waits to see
if good decisions or falls become your norm.
Sometimes, the Guardian Angel must sit back
and wonder what it is protecting you from.
Sometimes, the best protection it can give you
is to let you have the falls and get the hurts
so you will learn how to make better choices.

Guardian Angels can't be everywhere at all times.
If there are too many missteps to foil, then
tiredness, disappointment and confusion set in
on whether to keep picking you up
or to let you handle your problems yourself.

(continued)

Each bruise the Guardian Angel takes protecting you
deflates its energy and ability to help you further.

As you grow, the Guardian Angel must begin to
step back and accept the results of your actions and choices.
If you impose self-destructive behaviors on yourself,
the Guardian Angel can only cry when it sees
what it has tried so hard to prevent.

Eventually the Guardian Angel must move on,
get out of the way and accept what is, thereby becoming
a still voice of conscience in the soul of the one
it so loves and wants so much to help.

A Guardian Angel no more!

Thoughts: Help yourself • Learn from mistakes • Appreciate help

H *Pp. 97-111*

□ habits

Habits
are fences we build
to keep us on familiar ground.

HANDS **(n.) - body part to reach out, influence**

hands

Hands that care
  gently reach out to pull up with love.
Hands that control
  forcibly reach out to dominate and influence.
Hands that hate
  angrily reach out to grab and hurt.
Hands that help
  purposely reach out to support and show interest.
Hands that are sad
  longingly reach out
    to find others to commiserate with them.
Hands that are lonely
  may not reach out at all
    or will desperately grasp at anyone offering.
Hands that are fearful of intimacy
  tentatively reach out
    but quickly pull back if others get too close.

Be aware of which hands are reaching out to you
  and to which hands you are reaching out.

Thoughts: Motives • Being influenced • Seeking others

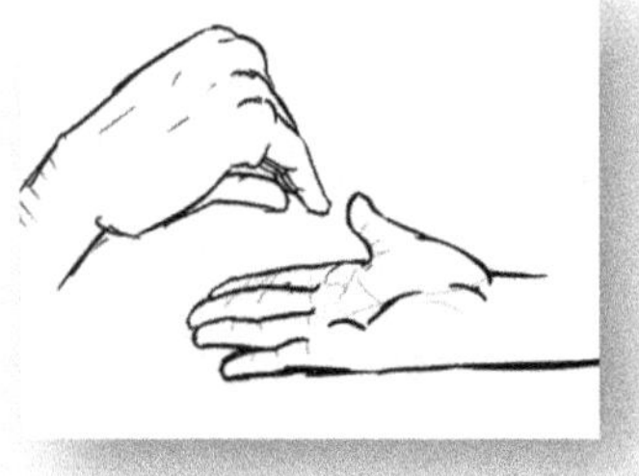

hands: Give & Take

☐happy

happy

I know I'm happy!
I'm at peace with myself!

If you're weary of the dreary
  and tired of being sad or mad,
    try exuding a positive attitude
      to get rid of feeling bad.
Smile for a little while and put on a happy face.
  Think of the pleasant and upbeat
    to help change the pace.
You may not feel less serious
  or chase all your blues away,
    but if even for an instant,
      you'll lighten your load for today.

Source: P. 15

HAPPY-SONG **(n.) - brings a feeling of pleasure or contentment**

happy-song

song

How can I cheer up this mood I'm in
and chase the blues away?
How do I make it happen to me?
What can I do? What can I say?

Sing a happy song.
Smile your blues away.
Hum a cheerful tune
and change your frown with laughter.

Don't let gray clouds cover that grin.
Just keep thinking what a happy mood you're in.

Sing a happy song.
Let your burdens soar.
Hum a cheerful tune.
Be happy ever-more.
It's that simple, just set the pace.
Let your smile lighten up your face with sunshine.

Sing a happy song.
Chase your cares away.
Lift your burdens with a tune.
Smile, whistle, laugh a lot.
You can do it now.
Just sing a happy song.

Thoughts: Change your mood • Think happy thoughts

HATEFUL-SPEECH (n.) - offensive speech against others

hateful-speech

Hateful-Speech: *Recipe:*

Accuse, be rude, be mean. Distort and show anger
to capture attention, incite, change the subject
and evade rational answers.

Avoid, divert and ignore rather than discuss or inform.

Be autocratic and loud to drown out truth
and give the impression of leadership.

Be dramatic, perform. Substitute rambling for eloquence
to get the highest reaction from the least informed.

Identify *"I"* as the authority for right
and *"THEY"* as the scapegoat for wrong.

Speak fast, be repetitive and simplistic rather than
explain or give time for careful analysis or thought.

Use accusations, generalities, innuendo,
opinions, slogans and stereotypes
to distract from and to substitute for the facts.

Use accuracy, courtesy, facts and truth ONLY when
no other expedient recourse is available.

Let it all bake in the hottest emotions possible,
then force-serve it to those who are eager
to believe and consume it.

Thoughts: Lack of integrity • Image vs. real • Ignorance • Take advantage • Prejudice • Self-serving

"*HELLO*" (interjection) - polite greeting to get attention

hello

"Hello and how are you?" (I really don't care.)
It's just my way of saying I see you there.
When you ask me the same thing
and I say *"Just fine,"*
it's just that I want to respond and be kind.

Wouldn't it be better if we really did care
how each of us feels and really be sincere?
But in this busy world full of strain,
we often only speak to each other for gain.
We'd rather just recognize that each other exists and
forego the real feelings that we knowingly miss.
We find it quicker and far easier too
than *'me'* being involved in making
a difference in *'you.'*

But when I am lonely, and hurting and sad,
I really would like to stop feeling so bad.
Knowing you're there and you see me as real
does give me a lift in whatever life deals.

So thank you for greeting me and saying *"Hello."*
I see you too as off we both go
to face the next encounter and the need to push,
so sorry to find that we always must rush.

Perhaps there will come a moment to care
and to help each other each time we are there.
And when that time comes, how good it will feel
to know that the interest and greetings are real.
Then will come strength to face what comes next,
and do it with hope that it will be for the best.

(continued)

"Hello and how are you?" **I really am fine.**
I hope that you're feeling as good as I'm.
I really do care about how you're feeling inside you
and really appreciate your caring about me too.

Thoughts: Gracious greetings • Important to care

□help

Helping others helps us to stop worrying about ourselves.

If you can't help, get out of the way to make room for others who can.

Some furiously tread in deep treacherous water
trying desperately to stay afloat.
Yet they wave graciously and smile warmly
to those who pass by rather than ask for help
or let anyone know they are in trouble.

I need:

My belief in myself restored.

My dreams refreshed.

My hopes rekindled.

Can someone please help?

□here

Sometimes we find we are
ALL HERE
because we're not
'ALL THERE!'

HIGH (n.) *(slang)* - euphoric condition
induced by drugs

high

You opiate yourself into a dreamlike stupor.
Walls of smoke and thought-altering chemicals
envelop your brain, dull your senses
and blur your vision of the world.
Like an ephemeral Band-Aid,
you cover the hurts sustained
in your waking hours

High above cares and reason,
you experience basic pseudo-pleasure:
Hurts repressed.
Pain forgotten.
Tensions deadened.

Loud pulsating music blurs your reality.
You sit in your own little capsule,
a world of your own making,

Hours of dreamlike calm go by,
but each minute pulls back
the curtain enfolding you letting in
the light of reality once more.

Your eyes squint against the spotlight of truth.
Your head throbs from the rousing overture
signaling the new day.

(continued)

Slowly the curtain is open completely,
and you are at stage-center of life again.
You make up with the appropriate expression
needed to face the day.
You determinedly play your role
for the audience around you
hoping to dodge the criticism of a bad act.
You seek applause and recognition
for your performance
not for the person you could be.

As the lights of your day dim,
you return to your private world
to forget, shut out and hide.
You bring back your curtain to seal off your world
high above those who give you pain.

Thoughts: Reasons for escape • Addiction & its costs

high: Hiding from reality

HOLIDAY-SEASON (n.) *(slang)* - From Thanksgiving to New Year's Day

holiday-season

It's the holiday season around us again this year.
It's that brighten-up reason,
a time for happy greetings and cheer.

It's that holiday season, one more time.
So pack up troubles and put away tears,
sparkle smiles on everyone near
'cause that special holiday season is here.

It's a time for making merry. It's a time for feeling good.
It's a time for singing and doing nice things
for all the people you should.

It's the holiday season around us again this year.
It's that stepping out season,
a time for lots of laughter and cheer.

It's that holiday season, one more time,
with snow that is glistening,
candles-a-flickering,
bells are a-jingling now.
'Cause it's that holiday season again this year!

song

□hope

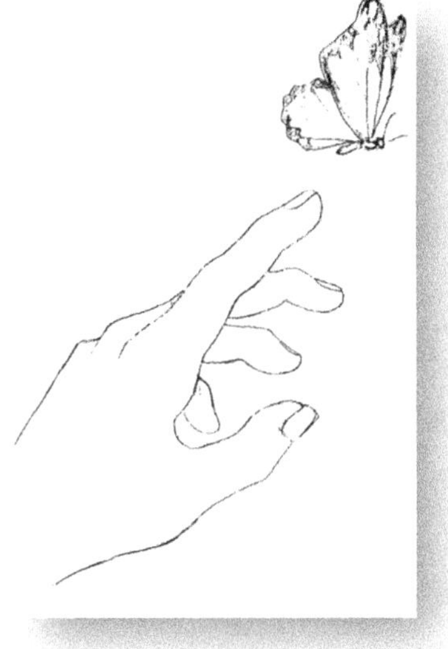

hope: Just beyond reach

Hope
A fluttering butterfly,
visible, but just beyond reach.
Source: P. 108

Hope:
A fragile guideline
to an unseen target.
Source: P. 108

To hope
is not the same
as to do!

HOPE **(n.) - a feeling that what is wanted will happen**

hope

Invisible stairs
leading through clouds of dreams
to imperceptible heights.

A fluttering butterfly,
visible, but just beyond reach.

A fragile guideline
to an unseen target.

An internal strength
to be called forth
to support impossible weights.

A belief, prayer, wish.

A priceless treasure
at the end of a far distant rainbow.

An indefinable feeling
that says everything.
is going to be all right.

Thoughts: Hope vs. reality • Importance of hope

☐hugs

Hugs
magically sprinkle an aura of stardust
on the psyche.
They squeeze out
hurt, loneliness, worry and fear
from the heart and mind of the recipient
and fill the void with a feeling of
confidence, love, warmth
and well-being.

☐humor

Some people
disguise rudeness as humor.
But those who laugh with them
are party to perpetuating the offense.

☐hunter

hunter

HUNTER (n.) - one who searches carefully for something to capture and use

hunter

Finely tuned tunnel-visioned eyes
  carefully scope out possible sources of sustenance
    so as not to miss any feeding opportunity that comes.

With emotionless resolve, unfeeling heart
  and desensitized conscience,
    the hunter pushes forward on his deliberate mission.
Unashamed and determined,
  he has only one goal – *TO GET!*
His sharpened wits and dulled emotions
  enable him to target those from whom he can take
    as much as he can.

Truth buried under self-serving lies and plausible fantasies
  is directed at those who want to believe.
The goal is to leave them with
  some vestige of hope and good feeling
    about what they have been duped into giving.

Nothing given to him is ever enough
  to fill his insatiable needs.
His too little giveback is only a calculated offering
  designed to get more.

He allows no kindness to be left unabused
  and no good deed to go unpunished.
He quickly excretes, as undigested by-products
  of his manipulation and guile, the trust,
    caring and love sincerely given by others.

(continued)

Once his unsavory task is accomplished,
he brushes himself off from the encounter
and erases what he has done from his mind.
He leaves, never looking back,
uncomfortably content with where he is
and assuredly unsure of where he is going.

And so, the hunt goes on . . . .

Thoughts: Taking advantage • Selfishness • Unkind

□ hurting, hurts

Don't assume you have to
keep hurting yourself
just because you haven't learned
how to do anything else.

Pull out the daggers others left there!
Let the blood of past hurts flow.
It will stop! - Source: P. 74

You can't see my hurts. They don't show.
But you can hear them in my words,
understand them in my attitude
and realize them in my actions.

If we let the fire of past hurts linger,
the residual smoke can blind us
from seeing our way forward.

☐icing

icing: Oops

ICING (n.) - sweet frosting on top of a cake

Icing

Icing to an unscrupulous baker
  is like giving to a convincing taker.
The sweet facade covers what he wants to hide
  with a distracting confection of illusion.

Fluff and glitter, so visually appealing,
  camouflage defects and conceal the truth
    of the flawed creation underneath.
One must look under the fluff to understand
  the true essence of what actually is.

(continued)

Disguising what has little value
by using imagination and flair can't replace
integrity and reality nor transform
an inadequate cake into a quality confection.

The sweet concoction and glitter so visually appealing
can overwhelm the taste buds of protection
and be swallowed without understanding
by a trusting and unsuspecting consumer.

The pleasant aftertaste can't substitute for quality for long.
Eventually, a connoisseur of truth will realize
he's been had by an amateur that's bad.

But when sweet icing is used to artistically compliment
a carefully created quality cake underneath,
what looks and tastes great will be joyfully anticipated
and really enjoyed as it lives up to expectations.

Why expend effort and skill to create a deceptive illusion
when you can fix rather than disguise flaws, and perfect
rather than dress up what has little substance?

Why not share with dignity your best efforts
and show what you can actually accomplish
rather then conceal a lack of care, integrity or skill?
Then tasteful icing, glittering sprinkles
and eye-catching fluff will enhance a proud creation
rather than just cover up flaws.

Always frost with truth, glitter with integrity
and sprinkle with dignity to serve
appreciative and trusting others your very best.

Thoughts: Image vs. reality • Quality vs. show • Integrity

IF **(conjunction) - what could happen**

If

If you want,

Act!

If you want back,

Be worthy!

If you need,

Earn!

If you love,

Give!

If you hope,

Plan!

If you value,

Protect!

If you care,

Show it!

Thoughts: Make things happen • Go for it!

□impulses

To restrain reckless impulses, use your:

Conscience **as your side view mirrors.**

Memory **as your rearview mirror.**

Morals **as your restraining seat belts.**

□indulgence

Insatiable needs
are never satisfied
by excessive indulgence.

☐ inner-child

To give your inner-child your attention
and keep it feeling protected and safe,
your mature adult self needs to emerge
from the cocoon of self-indulgence.
Then you can soar to beautiful new heights
and face whatever challenges await.

INTERACTION (n.) - communication, working together

Interaction

Please treat me nicely with
soft words, kind deeds and pleasant actions.
Please handle me gently with caring thoughts,
sunshiny glances and loving embraces.
Please consider my feelings with careful comments,
sincere smiles and thoughtful reactions.

Please honor me with understanding by
attention to my presence,
recognition of my intrinsic worth and
acknowledgment of my being.

Listen to my words not just hear the sounds.
Look at me not through me.
Speak to me not at me.

I think, feel, hope and dream.
I want, care, perceive and understand.

(continued)

Appreciation
  makes me feel needed.
Attention
  makes me feel I exist.
Being needed
  convinces me I have purpose.
Kindness
  makes me feel special.
Praise and recognition
  help me feel worthy.

I need warmth to chase cold,
  comfort to ease pain,
  sunshine to replace blues,
  ups to balance downs.

I'm a person!
  Please remember
    and act accordingly!

Thoughts: Communication skills • Kindness • Positive interaction • Give attention

□job

*A job well done
is a job well done!
Nothing else needs to be said.*

☐joke

A cruel joke that hits home
is at first a pinprick
that startles our attention
and stimulates automatic laughter.
Too many such jokes become painful stabs
that expose our sensitivity,
numb the humor
and trigger an internal ache
that cries out for relief.

☐justice

Our view of justice for those
who do not meet our expectations
is for them to suddenly realize
the error of their ways
and beg our forgiveness
or get their *'just rewards.'*
('just rewards' = punishment we think someone deserves)

☐kind (adj.)

Some people
need an interpreter
to understand
kind actions and words.

KIND (adj.) - considerate, friendly, generous
KINDNESS (n.) - being kind

Kind

A kind word
is an unexpected lighting bolt of energy that:
Flashes brightly.
Lights up the darkest mood.
Reinvigorates awe.
Shocks us to attention.
It leaves as quickly as it came,
but fond remnants remain
embedded in our memory.

A kind smile
is the guiding beacon
from a welcoming lighthouse
that appears suddenly
and illuminates the isolating darkness.
It encourages safe steering
away from gloomy uncertainty
and opens the way to a confident journey.

A kind gesture
is an act of goodness,
like a benevolent monarch
choosing you from the anonymous crowd
to wear the regal robe.

Thoughts: Be kind • Be thoughtful •
Appreciate kindness

☐kindness

Kindle the buried flame of kindness in others
by igniting your own spark
and warming the world around you.

Source: P. 33

When kindness touches a troubled spirit
with its comforting uplift and warmth,
it can be a sweet respite
for an appreciating recipient.

TO SOME, KINDNESS RECEIVED
IS A BLESSING TO BE APPRECIATED.
TO OTHERS, KINDNESS GIVEN
IS A SIGN OF WEAKNESS
TO BE EXPLOITED TO THE FULLEST.

KNOW (v.) - be aware from observing or information

Know

One who knows the depths
can really appreciate the heights.
One who has felt hurt
can sincerely offer healing,
One who has been the victim
can truly savor victories.
One who has experienced pain
can honestly share empathy.
And one who understands rejection
can fully know the importance of acceptance.

Thoughts: Understanding • Experience Counts • Sensitivity

☐ labels

Labels can influence others
and how they see us.
But we can overcome
as long as we don't believe
what we know is not true.

Source: See P. 157

labels

□ late

It is never too late to make up for wrongs,
but it is also never too early.

LATE (adv.) - not on time;
- beyond appropriate time

late

I could have . . . .
I might have . . . .
I should have . . . .
I would have . . . .
I wanted to . . . .
I wish I had . . . .
But I didn't!

I thought about . . . .
I wondered if . . . .
I believed, hoped for and expected.

I look back and see
what could and should have been.
If only I could change what has passed
then things could be different.
But I can't.
It's too late!
Or is it?

Thoughts: Do rather than wish • Better late than never

LATER (adv.) *(slang)* - *"See you later;" "Never"*

later

Do you understand now?
I told you not to get involved.
I told you to give up and forget me.

I know you wanted to help!
You gave, and I took.
I wasn't very nice to you.
I didn't even try to give back.
I didn't do what you wanted me to do.
I lied, was rude, did things to hurt.

I guess I appreciate what you did.
You did help! You know that don't you?
You tried to guide me, but I didn't listen.
I couldn't be what you wanted me to be.
There was nothing more you could do!

What did you expect?
I want to do what I want to do!
I don't know where I'm going,
but I want to get there fast.
I hear advice, but I won't listen.
I rip off those who give to me
and give to those who rip me off.

I push away anyone who cares
so it's one less person I can hurt.
I can't do anything so it turns out right.

Maybe I do want help
to erase the mistakes I shouldn't have made;
to build up what I tried for so long to destroy.

(continued)

I'm in too deep, too far under, too far gone.
I'm a square peg in a round hole:
Not fitting in. Never knowing where I belong.
Always wondering if everything is my fault.
Always hoping, searching and waiting
for things to get better.

I dream, but I awake to nightmares.
I hurt so badly, it doesn't hurt any more.
I run! I don't know why or where!

I looked outward for help.
I looked inward for help.
Finally, I just stopped looking.

So here I am!
Nowhere! Nobody! Nothing!
A personless person.
Hopelessly hoping.
Eagerly destroying
what should never have been.

Why do you believe I could really be somebody?
Why not just go along with
what everybody else thinks of me?
Maybe I really am what they see.

Please stop caring.
Don't be disappointed. Just give up!
Then I can't hurt you any more or
bring you any more trouble, pain or grief.

L a t e r . . . .

Thoughts: Feeling hopeless • Pushing others away

LEAF **(n.) - part of a green plant**
that makes food for the plant

leaf

Patiently awaiting the sunlight
that shines and warms the world
for all to partake of,
each leaf twists, turns and faces upward
from its own unique position
to catch the available beams
not already taken by another.

A leaf is energized by
the magical kiss of sunlight's golden rays
shining on it alone.
It soaks up the radiant warmth
and basks in its glow,
satisfied for the moment,
yet always storing some in reserve
for those moments
when there will be no sunlight.

Thoughts: Attention • Planning • Sharing

□ learn

We must teach children
the SKILLS needed to learn,
the DESIRE to want to learn
and the BELIEF they can learn.

□lie

LIE . . .
A TIGHTROPE YOU WALK
ALWAYS FEARFUL OF THE FALL.
Source: P. 127

lie

Lie: A bullet aimed to blind, confuse, destroy, fool, hurt, pierce, scar and shock the receiver in a way that cannot be repaired or restored.
Source: P. 126

LIE (n.) - a false statement with intent to deceive

lie

A bullet
aimed to blind, confuse, destroy, fool, hurt,
pierce, scar and shock the receiver
in a way that cannot be repaired or restored.

A costume
suiting a particular role you want to play
even though you don't know the lines.

A clumsy erasure
of past difficulties, failures and problems
that can still be detected if you look closely.

A grease easing you into new situations
for which you are not ready to enter.

A key to a locked door that it doesn't fit.

A leaking life preserver in a sea of troubles.

A makeup
camouflaging the blemishes of past errors
that makes you look good
but only until it wears off.

A pattern of action created
that must now be followed
so you will not be discovered.

A premise
that you will be believed by others
who care, trust and have faith in you.

(continued)

A slipcover
  hiding the wear-and-tear of your life.

A ticket to a game
  for which you don't know the rules.

A tightrope you walk
  always fearful of the fall.

A tinted glass
  that shades reality.

A token on the bus of opportunity
  going in a direction for which
    you are unprepared to go.

A trap
  in which once caught,
    it now becomes your label.

A lie deceives others!
  But it deceives you even more!
    It was YOU that you weren't sure of!

Thoughts: Why lie? • Lying as a habit • Deception

lie: Camouflage

LIES (n.) - false statements with intent to deceive

lies

Lies are a crude language of disdain for truth
that honest people do not speak or understand.
The vocabulary is comprehensible,
but the meanings and intent defy logic.

Lies make up a foul and unscrupulous communication
that bypasses integrity.
The cadence is too quick
for immediate comprehension.
Inflections are used to misdirect.
Meanings are calculated to deceive.

Lies are a craftily woven fabric
of the seemingly rational
and the improbable but possible.

Lies are deliberate darts of deception
thrown without conscience, logic or respect
in order to tranquilize the victims' rational safeguards
and lure them into a lair of plausible fantasy.

Lies have a grammar of confusion,
a punctuation of irregular nuance and color
and a composition of avoidance.

Lies purposefully build on false foundations
on which rests the trusting but gullible judgment
of those who are taken in.

(continued)

Lies can start quickly and without careful thought,
but they take effort, perseverance
and a keen memory to maintain.

Lies can become habitual devices
that feel right and familiar to one who
has deftly practiced the deceptive craft
and whose conscience no longer hears
the sweet melody of self-respect and truth.

Those who survive on lies use them as:
A fuel to keep running from reality.
A mask to retain the made-up persona
they hide behind so others will believe it is real.
A road map to get them to where
they think they need to go.

The truth about lies is
that lies are NOT TRUE!

Thoughts: Consequences • Trust • Dealing with lies

□ life

Life is a:

Buffet of opportunities.

Potpourri of choices.

Smorgasbord of experiences.

Indulge!

Life is finding the right waves
and riding them in as far as you can go.

Life is lived in moments,
but judged in lifetimes.

Source: P. 130

LIFE (n.) - the existence of an individual

life

Life is like a blank sheet of paper given to us
to create our own personal work of art.
We can use it to
carefully draw or casually doodle;
meticulously write or randomly scribble.

Life is:
Crafted by talents used and opportunities taken.
Designed by choice and chance.
Inspired by hopes and dreams.
Produced by actions and skills.
Shaded by outlook, moods and perceptions.
Tinted by mistakes and successes
and displayed for all those who have interest.

Life is lived in the present
but can only be fully understood
when looked back on from the future.

Life is lived in moments
but judged in lifetimes.

Thoughts: Make meaningful choices • Take opportunities

☐ limits

Limits are restraints
that keep us free.

☐ listen

Some allow themselves to hear
only those who holler the *loudest,*
while others listen carefully to hear
those who speak the *softest.*

☐ lock

If you lock me out,
why would you expect me to still be there
when you open up again?

☐ loneliness

Loneliness is a deafening silence
waiting to be shattered by a caring voice.

Loneliness is the price some people pay
for not wanting to be hurt.

That loneliness is greatest
when we know there are those
who could ease it, but don't or won't.

Why are we lonely?
We are not alone?

Source: See P. 132

LONELY (adj.) - solitary or isolated;
- unhappy at being alone

lonely

Why am I lonely? I am not alone!
I see people all around me,
hundreds of people each day.

What am I looking for?
Someone to be nice to
and who befriends.
Someone to care for
and who accepts.
Someone to give to
and who appreciates.
Someone to talk to
and who answers.
Someone to trust and confide in.

I need contact with others
to complete the circuit
that creates that special charge
between giver and taker
allowing the current of acceptance to flow,
lighting up my world and
making me feel needed and wanted.

(continued)

Perhaps I can find someone
who responds, trusts and befriends,
but I'll still feel lonely.

Perhaps:
I don't feel worthy of acceptance, love or trust.
I don't believe I am likable.
I am unwilling to accept
that others could want to care.

Perhaps loneliness is inside:
Closed in. Walled off. Unable to break out.
Lonely!

Thoughts: Lonely or alone? • Being lonely in a crowd

lonely

LOSER (n.) - generally unsuccessful

loser

You are a contradiction:

You accept disappointment as permanent
but achievement as temporary.

You believe the worst about yourself
but expect the best from others.

You hope for success
but refuse chances to achieve it.

You magnify the insignificant
but minimize the good and positive.

You are satisfied with dissatisfaction.

You stay in the shadows
rather than show what you can do.

You want self-reliance
but look for support at every turn.

You want others to care
but push them away when they try.

You are willing to do the unthinkable
to get the useless.

You wish rather than do,
complain rather than correct,
cover-up rather than be truthful,
hope rather than plan.

You work at losing by
blinding yourself to opportunity;
choosing unproductive and unrealistic goals;
deafening yourself to helpful advice.

(continued)

You are someone who could but won't
change unproductive habits;
dare to make dreams come true;
learn from mistakes;
persevere when things get tough.

Why do you lose?
Because you make it impossible to win!

Thoughts: Change attitude • Take advice • Self-image

☐loss

Loss removes our sense of security
and leaves an exposed hole inside
that fills up with
raw feelings, resentments
and unanswered questions.

☐loudness

Loudness
does not increase
the accuracy of words.

Source: P. 37

□love

Love . . .
The nutrient
for a life to bloom
to its fullest.

Source: P. 141

love: In bloom

If affection is the bread
then love is the cake
and acceptance of that love
is the sweet frosting on top
to be mutually savored and enjoyed.

Love enters the world through:
Beautiful smiles.
Empathy and encouragement.
Nice words.
Simple kindnesses.
Small gestures.
Love is a soft place to put one's psyche.

Love gives to those it touches
the essence of human need:
***Courage, Hope, Meaning, Purpose* and *Strength*,**
and it returns to the giver
in a never-ending stream
as gentle rain, the end result of the cycle,
replenishes the depleted well.
Source: P. 141

Love:
ROOTS: *Mutual Trust and Safety.*
BRANCHES: *Self-confidence and Fortitude.*
FLOWERS: *Good Feelings and Pleasant Thoughts*
that bloom and inspire
Peace and Contentment.

Love . . .
A deep well of crystal clear pure water
waiting to nourish life
to enrich the parched soil of humanity
and give the very core of life
its sustaining source.

Source: P. 140

Love is a beautiful gift
when given with care and received with
graciousness and integrity.

Love given may not
reach its mark, have the desired effect
nor is it binding on the recipient
who may deflect, misuse or misunderstand it.

The greatest sadness of love
is when it is unavailable
to be given or received.

When love is ignored, misused or rejected,
it becomes the crumbs of our hopes and expectations
that we can either brush aside sadly and discard
or wistfully internalize and keep as an empty-calorie residue
that adds nothing nutritional or substantial
to our emotional palate.

LOVE: Requires a viable outlet
for it to be plugged into world goodness.

When love is successfully given and received,
it is an inspired connection that:
Energizes the soul.
Lights up the spirit.
Warms the psyche.

If misguided by the giver
or irrelevant to the intended,
love becomes a loose, exposed sputtering spark.

Its energy is drained off unused, leading nowhere,
leaving the depleted giver
disappointed, lonely and cold
with a large empty space in the soul.

love: Energy and power flows

LOVE (n.) - deep affection, attraction;
- feeling; liking for someone

love

A deep well
of crystal clear pure water
waiting to nourish life
to enrich the parched soil of humanity
and give the very core of life
its sustaining source.

With just a few drops:
Confidence blooms.
Faith springs forth restored.
Hope erupts.
Smiles form.
Warmth emerges.

The parchness of cares subsides,
the cracks and furrows of worry disappear
and haphazard and capricious scattering
in all directions gives way to
taking root and blooming
to one's fullest potential.

Love must be used properly.
It can nourish weeds
as well as exotic blooms.
It can flood and muddy
where no growth exists.
It can smother that which
cannot adapt to its depths.

(continued)

When love is given
  and touches another human being
    who absorbs and uses its powerful sustenance,
  the result is a replenishing of the spirit as the:
    Beauty of a rose enriches sight.
    Melodious song of the nightingale
      soothes hearing.
    Tartness of a fresh strawberry
      tingles the taste.
    Sweetness of honeysuckle
      stimulates smell, and the
    Soft cool grass pleases the touch.

Love gives to those it touches
  the essence of human need:
    Courage, Hope, Meaning, Purpose and *Strength*;
and it returns to the giver
  in a never-ending stream
    as gentle rain, the end result of the cycle,
      replenishes the depleted well.

Love
  Cares, Gestures graciously, Looks knowingly,
    Smiles warmly, Speaks kind words
      and Touches gently.

Love:
  Accepts that someone wants you to grow and develop.
  Knows someone is empathetically listening.
  Realizes that someone is aware you exist.
  Understands that someone cares.

Love:
  The nutrient for a life to bloom to its fullest.

Thoughts: Special feeling of love • Power of love

□low

Sometimes your lowest point can be your best viewpoint for seeking the path upward.

□macho

macho

MACHO (adj.) - masculine, brave, tough

Macho

Aggressive enough
  to accept from others.
Big enough
  to attend to small things.
Bold enough
  to show kindness.
Brave enough
  to show fear.
Capable enough
  to ask for help.
Confident enough
  to deal with change.
Macho enough
  to show gentleness.
Proud enough
  to show disappointment.
Secure enough
  to handle failure and loss.
Strong enough
  to show weakness.
Tough enough
  to show restraint.
Virile enough
  to show affection.

Thoughts: Character strength • Caring • Sensitivity

MAN **(n.) - a human being; a person**

man

Animal:

eat	-	*drink*	-	*taste*	-	*smell*
copulate	-	*groom*	-	*grow*		
move	-	*run*	-	*hide*	-	*play*
satiate	-	*sleep*	-	*die*		

Physical survival through:
Instinct.
Physical satisfaction.
Self-preservation.

Human:

blush	-	*smile*	-	*weep*
change	-	*create*	-	*enjoy*
plan	-	*decide*	-	*prepare*
respect	-	*trust*	-	*believe*
think	-	*speak*	-	*understand*

Survival of the spirit through:
Changing direction.
Influencing surroundings.
Overcoming seemingly insurmountable obstacles.
Building a life based on purpose, planning and good intentions.

man

MARIONETTE (n.) - puppet; controlled from above by strings

Marionette

An animated performer
with an impish grin and easy laugh
tiptoes along a scripted path
taking cues from whatever impresses others.

Trapped in its own spotlight,
it can not reach out
for independence and self-control.
It charms others
by casting an aura of stardust on the psyche,
but only sees itself
as the distorted funhouse mirror image
of a street urchin who can not please or succeed.

It is controlled by
the strings of others' opinions
and by a desire to never disappoint or displease.
A freckle-faced Huck Finn,
it is adrift in a world
in which it is anchored in awe.

And so it remains the performer
unable, unprepared and unready
to independently navigate the tides
of grown-up responsibility and personhood.

Thoughts: Independence • Making Choices • Always wanting to please others

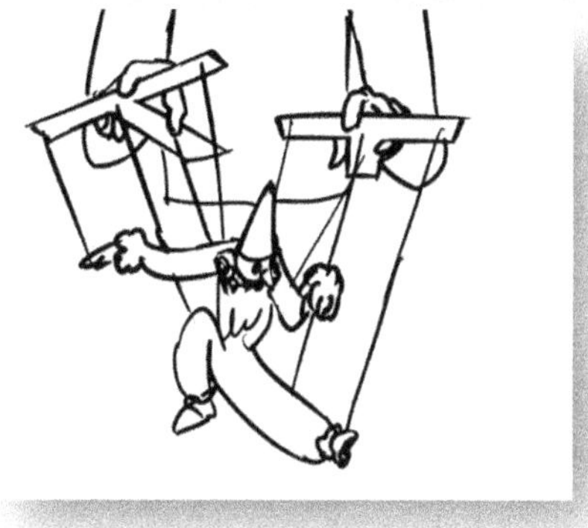

marionette

☐ maturity

Maturity

is moving further and further away

from the security of the familiar

and into the realm of uncertainty.

☐ memories

Memories . . .
a storeroom of used but precious moments
to be recalled and relived
when we but wish to open the door.

Source: P. 148

The flavor of delicious memories
as well as hard-to-swallow lessons of the past
create the foundation
from which all future grows.

Source: See P. 184

MEMORIES (n.) - things stored in our subconscious
that we remember

memories

A storeroom
of used but precious moments
to be recalled and relived
when we but wish to open the door.

A magic carpet
releasing us from the present
and flying us to past moments
that envelop us in pleasure.

A computer link
to selected perceptions and images from the past
in any order and to fulfill any purpose.

A closet of clothes
to enter at will and try on meaningful items.
Sometimes the fit will be different
from what we remember,
or the images not what were hoped for.

A gauze we can see through to:
Ease harshness, ugliness and flaws.
Dull sharpness and vividness. Enhance beauty.

A party
to which we invite those we want,
create the setting and be our own guest.

A treasure
with an aura of specialness
that only we can fully appreciate.

(continued)

A window
enabling us to see as far back
as hindsight will allow.

Memories can:
Erase reality
if we are too selective.
Flood our thoughts
if we dwell on them too much.
Obliterate the present
if we depend too heavily on them.
Sadden or burden us
if we worry over what might have been.

Memories preserve our view of the past
that no one can remove or take away from us.

Memories are our own private world
that only we have and are ours forever
to keep, cherish and treasure.

Thoughts: The past is part of us • Perspective

☐mending

Mending
can stop things from ending!

☐mirror

Some look in a mirror but can only see
reflected back a funhouse mirror distortion
of all those beautiful and special qualities
that are really there. **See image: P. 189**

MISSION (n.) - a journey with a specific purpose;
(*slang*) - going out to get drugs

Mission

Brilliant sunshine bottled up
within an unsuspecting host.
A warm, strong, charismatic presence
so easily visible to others who,
once touched by the magical kiss
of innate quality, beauty and dignity,
are transformed into energized beings
never able to settle for the ordinary again.

Christmas morning eyes
excitedly view the world with childlike anticipation.
Face pressed close to the windows of the world,
he vicariously observes all that impinges on the senses
trying to sort out the complex tapestry of society.

Never quite finding that elusive key to enter mainstream
to convention, stability or a sense of belonging,
he is always on the outside fringes
like a quiet prowler agilely cat-pawing through
the shadowed alleys and dingy corners of life.

Dredging the refuse for acceptance and survival, he displays
an attractive facade to entice anyone who will come,
letting darkness shield the indelible scars
and devastating insecurities ingrained inside.

This once soft fragile seashell gradually burdened down
by mistakes, bad habits and self-doubt
has become encrusted with unbearably heavy barnacles
of failure, guilt and self-abuse.

(continued)

Forced to rock bottom,
he is unable to rise and overcome for fear
he will burst and self-destruct at a higher level.
This now transformed deep ocean-like creature
is out of reach of the warmth, support and
penetrating reality of daylight needed for growth.

Lost, misplaced, alone and out of his normal habitat,
he must toughen and adapt to the
dark, murky environment into which he has sunk.
He is left scavenging the inhospitable and dangerous
bottom for basic sustenance and breath
and must fight to survive the never-ending onslaught
of forceful uncaring undercurrents
that keep him ominously rushing through
torrents of travail, despair and confusion.

He eagerly grabs at any attractive lure
that might offer momentary respite or security,
afraid to miss any chance to be swept away
from the pressured present.
Disregarded are the conditions, consequences
and effects that are hidden under
its titillating and deceptive camouflage.

Once hooked, he determinedly clings like a beggar
accepting crumbs and abuse from anyone going past
and goes off in the direction pulled, satisfied
to do whatever will gain a few more moments
of survival along the painful drift to nowhere.

Momentary hopes to rise above the reality of the present
are injected in needle-sharp assaults of artificial courage
on the fragile core of feelings still left inside.

(continued)

The power surge produces a rush to great highs like
that of an impetuous trapeze artist without a safety net
blindly leaping from a euphoric launching pad,
groping for acceptance, escape and exhilaration.

From afar, out of reach and unable to help,
caring spectators watch the desperate performance
designed to fool no one,
and sadly leave rather than see the
inevitable crash back to the solid ground of reality.

Coming down plunges more hurt, guilt and scars
on the already burdened pile
of frustration, broken hopes and pain.
Yet the bone-searing fatigue
and the uncontrollable despair and confusion are
once more repressed in the irrational, unexplainable
and futile search for an even greater high
to punctuate the again hurting present.

Inside, the still repairable self-starting mechanism
lies shaken and rusted from self-doubt and misuse.
It still hopes for just one spark of self-control
to ignite the power left to move it out of
the destructive and self-defeating cul-de-sacs
of crashes, dead-ends and drifting
in which it is trapped.

The first wobbly strokes upward
will need strength and self-confidence
to wrest control from the pulls and influences
penetrating and holding him captive.

(continued)

Then the ascent to manageable heights once started
will carry the multifaceted precious treasure
buried deep inside through the fresh currents of
crisis-free decisions,
honest relationships
and free and careful choice,
and into the clear streams of achievement
and good feeling.

The launch from the immediate to the possible
leaves behind the merciless tides and pressures
that have held him prisoner to the destructive past.

Thus a confusing journey,
begun in self-indulgence,
lost in loneliness, self-doubt and rejection,
battered by lack of self-confidence,
destructive habits and bad influences,
is now back on course toward
self-control, renewed self-image and growth.

A new mission begins
buoyed by the applause and sighs of relief
from those waiting so long
for the return they hoped could come.

Change,
just an attitude away!

*Thoughts: Power of addiction • Change & Choice •
Recovery vs. not starting*

☐ moderation

To the compulsive,
  EXCESS is not enough.
To the self-controlled,
  MODERATION is more than sufficient.

☐ momentum

The impetus and momentum
to move ignored,
I remain where I was, at rest,
undaunted with my encounter to change.

Source: P. 68

MONEY **(n.) - cash, currency, wealth**

money

I like you!
You get me things that
are beautiful,
fill my wants and needs,
give me comfort
and sustain me.

You get me to places I want to go;
get me whatever I want whenever I want it;
give me time for leisure pursuits;
help me look the way I want;
help me meet others I want to know.
Through you, I am in control!

(continued)

I don't feel well!
  Can't you help me?
I'm lonesome!
  Can't you do something?
I'm afraid!
  Can't you change it?

What happens if
  I don't have you anymore?
    What will I do?
    Where will I go?
    Who will help me?

Please, someone help me!
  I'll pay anything!
    Or isn't it money that I need?

Thoughts: Limits of money • Savings • Values

□ mood

Mood:
 A revolving stage
  with settings from sunshiny bright
   to dark and brooding
  and controlled by our perceptions
   of ourselves and of the world around us.

mood: Changes

MUSIC (n.) - vocal or instrumental sounds making pleasing expressions of emotion

Music

Don't let the stormy clouds gather.
Just put a happy face on.
And it's so simple to do it,
just start by singing this song:

We can make music. We can sing songs.
We can make happy melodies
to keep us humming all day long.

And we can make music
that keeps us tapping our toes.
Oh, we can make music. Wonderful music.
We can make music all day long.
song

music

N - O *Pp. 157-166*

NAMES (n.) - a word or phrase by which
a person is known; often abusive

names

Why did they call me that?
I don't accept it! I don't like it!
They are wrong!

Why do I let words hurt me?
Unkind words are paper darts.
They can neither pain nor wound.
They hurt only if I let them
penetrate my ego
by lowering my belief in myself.

Labels can influence others
and how they see me.
But I can overcome
as long as I don't believe
what I know is not true.

Words designed to hurt?
I hear you,
but I won't listen!

Thoughts: Why do names hurt? • Positive nicknames

☐ **need**

Do not confuse
NEED with GREED!

We need
to be needed.

☐ **negative**

Avoiding the positive
is NEGATIVE!

NICE (adj.) - pleasant, caring, gracious

nice

One who cares about others' feelings, hopes, dreams, thoughts, opinions and well-being.

One who believes that others are important and worthy of consideration.

One who does for others to help, guide and be kind.

One who acts as if others also care, do kind things and are nice.

One who can't understand when others don't care, don't do kind things and are not nice.

Thoughts: Care about others • Also be kind to yourself

☐nice-guys

So when some say that nice-guys
always seem to finish last,
perhaps what they really mean to say
is *"Niceness always lasts!"*

Source: P. 161

nice-guys: Help others

NICE-GUYS (n.) - informal term for kind, compassionate males

Nice-guys

We're told that nice-guys finish last,
but I really can't accept it.
Perhaps those who keep saying that
exaggerate a bit!

It's true that nice-guys may lag behind
in races where deception
builds crooked paths that deviate
from decent values in conception.

Honorable folks just can't compete
when a few others change rules at will.
Keeping pace with nasties then
becomes a very bitter pill.

When we think of competition,
we all should be on the very same track
with goals and rules fixed in honor
and values that do not crack.

So there are times when nice-guys
seem to finish behind the cheats
who lie and make life grim for us
while appearing outwardly sweet.

But nastiness does not endure,
and cheating usually loses,
because no one wants to have a friend
who is always giving bruises.

(continued)

In the long run, the pace of honor
  for those caring to do what's right
will enable them to finish ahead
  of those looking for a fight.

While nice-guys do try to finish first,
  they sometimes let those who rush
go ahead when the field is crowded
  with those creating such a crush.

Nice-guys will help the stumblers
  and are often taken for granted,
because others know that nice guys are there
  for those who may get stranded.

Being nice and honorable
  makes for a slow and steady stride,
as they ignore those who may prosper
  but who aren't nice and have no pride.

Nice-guys know they can't always pace
  with the cheaters who are rotten;
but those who work at being nice to all
  can never be forgotten.

So when some say that nice-guys
  always seem to finish last,
perhaps what they really mean to say
  is ***"Niceness always lasts!"***

Thoughts: Caring • Thoughtfulness • Character

☐ niceness

Niceness to the selfish and ungrateful
  is fuel for their taking advantage.

NIGHT (n.) - darkness; opposite of day

Night

Turn on the night!
  Let me lose myself in its thick darkness
    as it surrounds me, engulfs me and
      swallows me up in its delicious anonymity.

I hide in daylight's crowded cage;
  but with night comes silence, aloneness and peace.
As night falls, I become emboldened and energized.
  Night cloaks us in our own radiance
    allowing the light of our inner selves to shine.

Night flows in gently covering the dirt of the day.
  It casts shadows on my faults
    while embellishing my self-image.
  It conceals my insecurities and flaws so visible
    and washes away my insignificance.

Night removes the spotlight shining on me
  and replaces it with a protective cover
    that stops the world from closing in.
It illuminates, magnifies and intensifies me
  allowing me to float to the top of my being.

Night frees my inhibitions to act.
  I become less on view and more able to be myself.
  I can move discretely and unrestricted
    as if suddenly released from the chains of daylight.
  I can observe without being noticed or standing out.
  I concentrate on the immediate and the close by.
  I can view less but focus more.

(continued)

Night?
I wait for you to cover me, hold me, keep me secure
and let me be myself as I want to be.

Thoughts: Anonymity • Night vs. day • Shadows

NO (adv.) - word used to refuse

no

"*No.*" I know it's a simple word.
Easily understood. Simple to say.
Uncomplicated to pronounce.

But if I say "*No,*" I might miss out
and not get to do what I want to do.
Besides, why should I be the only one saying it?
Why shouldn't I do what everyone else is doing?

It's not easy to say "*No.*"
Yes, I know I can cause myself problems,
get hurt, scar my reputation, get punished.
Even if I wanted to say "*No,*" it's hard.
I'm not going to be called '*chicken*' or '*baby!*'
I don't want anyone to think that I can't keep up!

I can take care of myself! I'll know when to stop!
Nothing will happen! Stop worrying! *Okay?*

Thoughts: Difficult to say "No" • Peer pressure • Consequences

Why didn't I just say *"NO?"*

Source: P. 54

"no": I didn't say it

NO! (interjection) - word used to give direction to stop

no!

"No!" said to children
often seems just a game.
We want to change what they do,
but they want to stay the same.

Children are perceptive and well understand.
They can *see* what you say,
and *hear* what you do.
They remember if you are consistent
and if what you say is true.

Children can always tell
when you don't mean what you say.
That's when you've lost the chance
that only comes with today!

(continued)

When *"No!"* is said to teach them,
then they must comply to learn.
If you don't follow through to reach them,
they could grow up and give you concern.

So when you say an important *"No!"*
mean it every time!
Then children can learn to respect your word,
and everything will be just fine.

Thoughts: "No!" means "No!" • Parent follow-through

☐nowhere

Why use the time that is
'Now Here'
to get
'Nowhere?'

☐obstacles

Obstacles
become stepping stones
when we accept problems
as challenges.

☐opportunity, opportunities

Opportunity:
A blend of disparate experiences
coming together by chance or choice
to create a masterpiece moment
of inspired connection
that can light your way in new directions.

When the ball of opportunity is thrown your way,
will you:
Catch it? Chase it? Watch it pass by?
Or let it fall wherever and go on your way?

Take each possible moment
and explore its opportunities.

THE MOST IMPORTANT THING ABOUT
AN **OPPORTUNITY** IS TO TAKE IT.

P *Pp. 166-187*

PAIN (n.) - physical suffering from illness or injury

Pain

Pain cannot be shared and is very hard to explain.
Whenever it is there, it's our individual burden to bear.

Pain can overwhelm our thoughts and attention
as we gasp for the breath of relief.
We may ask: *Why me? Why now? What to do?*
We can talk to ourselves with hope or in anger,
but limiting ourselves to self-talk is like a screech
on the echo chamber chalkboard of
our own limited world of experience.

Pain is exacerbated by isolation, fueled by worry,
inflamed by anger and prolonged by hopelessness.

Reaching out to caring others who allow us to share
can give us the welcome distraction of their interest.
Their concern can warm us as we absorb the balm
of their willingness to listen.
The healing caress of their empathy can give us
moments of joy within our hours of little relief.
Their soft touches of caring, affirming words
and wide eyes of focused attention can do wonders.
Their support can cushion us from our free fall into despair.
Their understanding can let us walk together
in our insight of the unexplainable.
Caring others are a treasure to be highly valued; and we too,
even in our pain, may also be able to help others cope.

Pain is not contagious, but some may act as if it is
and distance themselves when they see our distress.
Our suffering may cause discomfort to caring others who
must be allowed some respite so they don't need to pull away.
Those that should care but don't can make our cry for help
feel lost in a bottomless pit of indifference; so wanting,
hoping and waiting for them to change is of little value.

So what to do with our pain? We know that pain DOES hurt!
To react, we can complain, scream, wince and worry.
We can inflict anger on ourselves and others.
We can do our best to endure while seeking meaningful relief.
We can refocus our attention to give us tolerable moments.
We can work to confront and deal as best we can.
We can develop patience, self-reliance and even acceptance
to escape our feeling of helplessness.

Accepting the burden of pain may be possible if we:
Understand we are not alone in knowing pain.
Find meaningful help and support to address the cause.
Build up strength to acknowledge *'what is'* and look for ways to unblock our path to peace-of-mind from the intrusive, overpowering, debilitating obstacles in our way.

By seeking a way through or around our pain,
we may find understanding, hope and resilience.
Then, in spite of the daunting burden of our reality,
we may be able to find glimmers of opportunity
to once again tap into the world of joy and peace
that continues to shine around us.

Thoughts: Coping • Acceptance • Seek help & support

□ parent, parents

Parent:

◊ BE encouraging, firm, patient.
◊ BE kind, constructive, supportive.
◊ BE interested, helpful, caring.
◊ AND, BE THERE!

Parents
need to give their children
presence!

Eventually our parents
become our children.

☐ past, passed

The PAST
has already
passed.

How much better it is
to stop CRYING
about what has passed
and start SMILING
about what could come!

Source: P. 74 (See P. 214).

☐ paths

Some purposely take paths
filled with
Darkness, Detours, Obstacles and Potholes
so they don't have to reach
their declared destination.

Source: P. 49

☐ patience

Patients
need to have
patience.

PATIENCE (n.) - willingness to wait, if necessary, for what you want or need

Patience

The bread will not rise faster
if we look at it all day.
The seed will not flower
until it finds a fertile way.

The day will not go quicker
no matter how much wishing we do.
The amount of work you accomplish
still depends on you.

A damage stays until we find
a way to make it heal.
A problem left to vegetate
will never resolve a deal.

An artist paints in creative time
not moments on the clock.
Most goals can only be fully reached
in little steps and building blocks.

Time is very definitive
in hours, minutes and seconds.
Accomplishments do not readily gel
until the proper moment beckons.

(continued)

So patience, care and working toward
are things that must be done
if accomplishments, goals and races
are desired to be won.

Nothing good just happens,
and those who want too fast
need to learn that the waiting
justifies the time that passed.

For everything there is a time,
a place and way to do it.
So when a task seem impossible,
just plan the work to fit.

Give the bread its time to rise
and seeds their time to grow.
Remember anything you want to accomplish
needs to be worked for!

Now You Know!

Thoughts: "Patience is a virtue" • "Worth the wait"

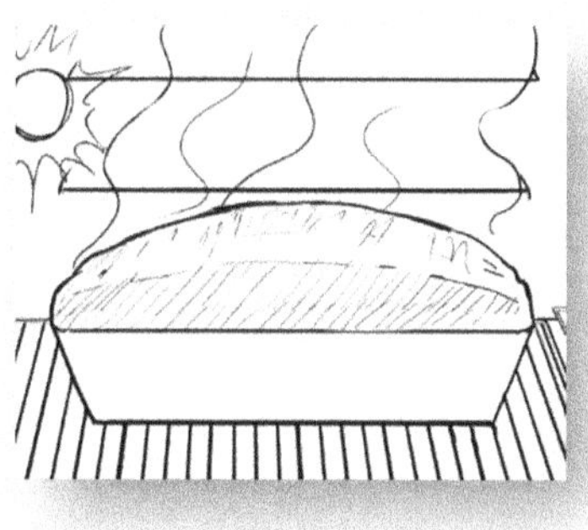

patience

***PEACE* (n.) - calm, harmony, order; freedom from war**

Peace

song

Maybe if we try hard enough
and dream and work together,
we could bring Peace to all the world
and really make it happen.

Let the world be filled with the sounds of music,
echoing everywhere.

Let each heart be filled with joy and hope,
a symphony of harmony.

Let the air be filled with children's laughter,
enough to change the world.

And let all the Earth be free from fear.
Let the world be filled with Peace.

peace

PETTINESS (n.) - undue concern with trivial matters;
- being spiteful, critical or mean

Pettiness

Pettiness is a blinder to reality:
It is seeing only what you want to see
and hearing only what you want to hear.

Pettiness is:
A dart aimed to hurt.

A depressant
to kindness, openness and sensitivity.

A dye aimed
to leave a stain for others to notice.

A splinter
aimed to irritate.

A stimulant
to dissension and discomfort.

It is the substance of small minds,
limited vision and uncaring hearts.

It is wrapped in ugliness
and sent with malice.

The receiver may leave it unclaimed.
Then only a slight residue of pity
for the sender will remain.

Thoughts: Why be petty? • Pettiness hurts others

PINBALL **(n.) - a game; you score as you hit targets and avoid obstacles**

Pinball

We are like the pinballs in a machine.
We are shot out forcefully.
We hit *'poles'* that happen to be in our way,
and they channel our path.

Barriers light up as we go along.
Some stop us from moving on;
others allow us to proceed with caution.
Some flip us off in directions we don't want to go;
others bounce us back to where we started.
Some delay us from reaching our goal;
others reward us for getting as far as we did.

Eventually our time runs out,
and we must take score of what we were able to do.

Thoughts: Lose / win • Skill vs. chance • Perseverance

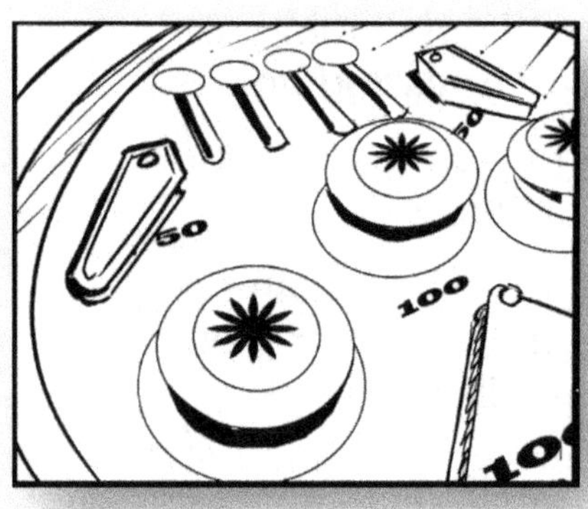

pinball

PLAN (v.) - to consider before doing

Plan

I do not understand people
   who buy shoes that are too small
nor comprehend why anyone
   would use foul language words at all.

It boggles my mind to think that folks
   with such a multi-choice of foods
buy things that couldn't possibly be
   any more nutritious than wood.

Some buy fast-foods and instant dinners
   and microwave them fast,
then complain about being bored
   and the time they have to pass.

To make hair look different,
   people fry, and bake and prune
that which nature gave them
   to care for not to ruin.

Why burn your skin in sunlight
   to get a darker shade
then have to accept the pain and suffering
   that your stupidity made?

We know that smoking hurts us,
   and drugs create devastation.
Yet use of both skyrockets
   even though we know
      our health's destination.

Why complain when aches and hurts
   appear without any warning
when we already knew ahead of time
   they result from our foolish yearnings?

(continued)

The body has its special needs
    and to maintain it takes much care.
To destroy and hurt for effect and show
    doesn't get us anywhere.

The dropout rate from our schools
    continues at an alarming pace
even though the education is free
    and available as a great base.

We complain about the lack of jobs
    and the low pay some employers give,
but don't we have to start somewhere
    so we can begin to live?

Why do some react with rudeness
    when a kind word will do?
And why would you feel hurt by criticism
    that could really be useful to you?

We want results and appearances
    that suit our mental tastes,
but the damage and chaos we create
    can cause an unbelievable waste.

Common sense and the practical
    take time and careful thought.
The fads, the ads, the faster things
    do not usually pay off.

Today is just a stop away
    from results that appear tomorrow.
So take care of today as insurance
    against some later sorrow.

A little time spent in planning
    and in thoughtful consideration
can make a major difference in
    our future situation.

Thoughts: Common sense • Plan • Take care of you

PLAY (n.) - a performance

play (n.)

Many of us see others as actors in OUR play
in which WE create the script, plan the ending,
write the lines and make things happen our way.

We tend to forget that OTHERS see us in
the same terms, but as players in THEIR productions.

Meaningful relationships need
compatible roles and story lines
that run in the same direction.

When two people share a script
and emote complementary sentiments,
a positive relationship can occur
that respects each other's need to shine
in attention's spotlight.

Then real-life scenarios can truly result
in beautiful productions with happy endings.

Thoughts: Competing for attention • Respect differences

play

□pollution

So as I cough my way through the very dirty air
or dodge the acid raindrops falling on my hair,
I try to ponder how we devise a proper solution
to the very complex Man-Made Mess
of DANGEROUS POLLUTION!

Source: P. 180

***POLLUTION* (n.) - harmful or poisonous things put into the environment (air, water, land)**

Pollution

I understand why vegetables and fruits have pesticides,
and the fact of antibiotic milk can even be put aside;
but the chemicals in water and the pollution in the air
don't give me any confidence in those who put them there.

Landfills leak their sewage,
and waters foam with soap.
Air is often discolored
with coal and oil burned to soot.
I know that nature's master plan
did not include this waste
from man-made things that cannot blend
nor find a natural base.

If tiny traces of vitamins and small dosages of pills
can help me over time to cure some devastating ills,
then the things in water, food and air that I can not see
and that find their way to my insides —
don't they slowly damage me?

(continued)

But as if all this were not enough,
  I certainly am more than curious
why people choose to hurt themselves
  in ways that are so serious.

For example: Those who cloud with smoke
  their vital healthy lungs,
or foolish folks deviating tired brains
  with all sorts of crazy drugs;
and those who willingly choose to eat
  any artificially flavored sugar-coated mess,
and even pay good money for it
  to fool themselves no less!

Try figuring out those
  who constantly pour alcohol inside,
a poison all dressed up as class,
  just to make themselves able to hide.
They talk as if they're happy,
  but when they weave and fall,
they become pathetic creatures
  not in control of themselves at all.

Let's not ignore the sound explosions
  from so-called music sources,
nor exclude the visual images bombarding us
  into becoming brain-dead corpses.
Are we supposed to be vitalized
  in our thoughts and conscious actions,
or awakened from the deep sleep
  induced by these impactions?

(continued)

So we smear on colorful makeup
  to healthy-up our faces
while taking multivitamins felt needed
  to perk up our paces.
We add stimulants and uppers to our food and drink,
  then wonder why computers must help us do and think.

We want to make things happen quickly
  so we can appear to be at our best.
We let our fingers do the walking
  and keep our feet at rest.
Having so callously tampered with
  our bodies' natural course,
we have to keep the masquerading up
  so things will not look worse.

But I still believe that nature has
  it's way of making nice,
and hopefully we will heed the call
  and take some good advice.

Listen to your natural sense
  for things in moderation.
Be aware of those who try to sell us
  chemical devastation.

So as I cough my way through the very dirty air
  or dodge the acid raindrops falling on my hair,
I try to ponder how we devise a proper solution
  to the very complex Man-Made Mess
    of DANGEROUS POLLUTION!

*Thoughts: Pollution • Clean water & air •
Conservation*

POTENTIAL (n.) - undiscovered qualities or abilities

Potential

THE FLOWER: Sweet in odor and
beautifully cloaked in its envelope of color.
It waits patiently to be appreciated
for as long as its bloom and scent last.

THE MEDICINE: Able to relieve pain and suffering.
It waits to be helpful when used as needed.

THE RECORD: Holding creative sounds
to be released with the press of a button.
It sits patiently just waiting to be heard.

THE STATUE: A marble elegance of sculpted beauty.
It stares silently waiting to be viewed and enjoyed.

The FLOWER, MEDICINE, RECORD and STATUE
all have qualities that have much to offer, but only
if there are those willing to appreciate them.
But if unused or kept hidden,
the qualities they have are of little value.

The potential is evident,
but ONLY to those who choose to appreciate.

Thoughts: Appreciate quality • Look for potential

potential

POWER (n.) - strength, capability, energy

power

Your attention has the power
to push me to stage center
by shining your nourishing spotlight
of interest on me.

Your acceptance has the power
to build up my confidence and pride.

Your deeds have the power
to erase my deepest emotional scars.

Your faith in me has the power
to build up my damaged ego.

Your smile has the power
to warm my coldest of moods.

Your touch has the power
to heal my most severe hurts.

Your words have the power
to lift unbearable burdens.

Your caring has the power
to exit me out of my loneliness.

Thoughts: Believing in someone • Encouragement

□ practicality

Practicality results when
Idealism and *Realism* meet.

PREPARE (v.) - to make ready

Prepare

Summer is here, and it is beautiful!
The sun is warm and comforting.
The breeze softly wafts the fresh smell of flowers
in all directions. Thoughts are of the moment.

Winter is coming! It will be cold!
The warmth and comfort of Summer will disappear.
The sweet smell of flowers will be just a memory.
Prepare for Winter!
Store nourishment for sustenance.
Find shelter for protection.
Be ready for the difficult period when you cannot
move freely to seek comfort or satisfy needs.

Is not Youth our Summer?
The time to enjoy, be protected by others and feel safe?
To explore, experience and make mistakes?
To think of the moment's immediate gratification?

Youth is our time to prepare!
Experience and learning shelter us from future error.
Responsibility builds toughness for difficulties ahead.
The carefree days of Summer will remain as memories
for smiles and support in sad times and warmth in cold times.

Prepare for the reality of future responsibility.
Then a new and different Summer will come,
a Summer of self-reliance and maturity,
but only if we are prepared to survive the cold Winter!

Thoughts: Responsibility • Prepare for adulthood • Plan

PRESENT (n.) - now; this period of time

present

The present is center stage
with yesterday's experiences
providing our repertoire
of props, words and actions
for coping with the new.

Our present creates the foundation
from which all future grows,
but it must not preclude
the flavor of delicious memories nor
the hard-to-swallow lessons of the past.

When our present is preoccupied
with pain and hurt,
the positive past is dulled,
and a dreary tomorrow forebodes.

But when happiness and joy flood our present,
the negative past is obliterated
and a receptive future is signaled.

Thoughts: Can't change the past • Enjoy today

□ pride *(negative)*

Pride: An artificial wall
put up by an insecure individual
to hold up
an unnecessary ego.

PRIDE (n.) *(positive)* - good feeling of accomplishment
(negative) - excessively high self-opinion

pride *(positive)*

A Spark: Bright and glowing.
A Flame: Spreading and intensifying.
A Blaze: Hot, fiery and raging.

Consuming, all encompassing:
Boosting confidence.
Enlarging the smile.
Radiating joy and satisfaction.
Straightening the back.
Quickening the step.
Warming the heart.

An Ember: Not to be forgotten.
Just waiting to be stoked
and fanned once more.

Thoughts: Feelings of satisfaction • Being proud

☐ problem (s)

You don't solve a problem
by creating a new one.

Problems
cannot be subtracted from
by adding to them.

Get your problems
before they get you!

Every problem
can be dealt with.
The only question is HOW!

SOME PEOPLE ARE LIKE VELCRO.
THEY ATTRACT PROBLEMS
THAT ATTACH THEMSELVES
AND WEIGH THEM DOWN.

When a problem appears, we can:
Run from it and AVOID;
Run to it and CONFRONT;
Stand still and IGNORE.

WHAT comes our way
is not the problem.
It's HOW we react to it that is.

□ prudent

The long-term track of the prudent is better than the fast track of fools.

□ put-downs

Put-downs
are some people's way
of doing pushups.

put-downs

PUT-DOWNS (n.) *(slang)* - saying things that make fun of or belittle someone

Put-downs

Why do you put me down?
I don't like put-downs! I hate them!
You have no right to do it!
Don't you think I care what others say?
Don't you understand that I have feelings?
Can't you see that I get angry and feel bad?

I am who I am! I do what I do!
It's none of your business.
Don't hassle me!

I could say things back that you won't like.
Things that put you down.
Would you like that?
How would you feel?

Don't put me down! Please!
I can't handle it!

Thoughts: Words can hurt • Self-image • Bullying

☐ rainbows

I chase rainbows
They are so pretty!
I wonder what I would do
if I actually caught one?

Source: P. 28

rainbows: Chasing

☐ raindrops

Raindrops:
Inconvenient, unwanted
and considered useless when present.
Yet they are appreciated, desired and wanted
when the results they provide are not there.
Then they are missed.

☐ reality

When reality does not fit our fantasy,
we may believe injustice has occurred.

How strange that some see
FANTASY as *Reality.*
Maybe it's because they are so used to seeing
***REALITY* as Fantasy.**

reality: Or Fantasy?

RECIPE (n.) - ingredients for a particular outcome

recipe

Oodles of niceness.
Gobs of friendship.
Lots of belief, faith and hope.
Overflow of caring.
Pounds of kindness.
Unlimited doing and service.

A pinch of giggles.
A block of strength.
A cube of determination.
A dash of silliness.
A bunch of dignity, intelligence and quality.

Mix well to dissolve lumps of hurt and loneliness.
Add a great deal of class.
Stir in a batch of graciousness.
Bake well in the heat of experience.

Frost with love.
Sprinkle with beauty. Serve with joy.
Appreciate with thankfulness.

A creation to be enjoyed.
A person to be treasured.

1992 / B

□ recovery

Recovery is the sweet icing of possibility
covering the imperfections of mishandling
thereby salvaging a wasted life
from the depths of hopelessness.

Source: P. 191

RECOVERY (n.) *(slang)* - getting off drugs

recovery

Slow healing nightmares reel through
  a consciousness struggling to get out
    from the darkness of illusion
      and into the daylight of reality.

Like on a damaged ship towed into calmer waters,
  surrealistic flashes and pulsating sounds
    of yesterday's battles still echo.
  Excitement remembered from actions past
    makes the real world appear comparatively bland
      as control, rational choices and caution
        begin to replace habitual recklessness.

As the new reality gradually revives the will
  to fight for self-control, it rekindles sparks
    of appreciation for an ordinary life filled with
      the beauty of hope, the wonder of self-belief
        and the potential for change.

Untapped energy can now be used to cultivate
  subtle positive accomplishments rather than
    push a tired body beyond endurance.

Recovery is the sweet icing of possibility
  covering the imperfections of mishandling
    thereby salvaging a wasted life
      from the depths of hopelessness.

Thoughts: Scars of battle • Salvaging dignity • Change

REJECTION (n.) - refusing to accept

rejection

I see you. I know you exist.
I believe you are important.

You look nice. I'd like your attention.
I need someone to know I exist!
I need to feel like I matter to someone.
I'm hurting and feeling low.

Please notice me!
I'm nice. I try to look my best.
You would like me if you got to know me.
Come over and say hello!
We can get to know each other.

Why do you look everywhere but here?
Don't you see me? Don't I exist?
Aren't I important enough to notice?

Are you shy?
Maybe you need someone to notice you?
Maybe you are feeling low too?
Maybe you are thinking what I am?

I wonder if I should come over to you?
Will you be glad?
Or will you turn away and ignore me
and make me wish I had never tried?

I need my world brightened up!
Perhaps I can brighten up yours,
and then maybe it will reflect back on me!
Here I come!

Thoughts: Feeling unwanted • Cope with rejection

☐ rejection

Some, like unbloomed flowers,
grow in the darkness
of rejection and self-doubt.
Faced away from the sunlight
of real caring and attention,
they are unable to root
in that which nourishes self-worth
keeping their potential beauty and quality
undeveloped and undiscovered.

See P. 94

☐ relationship

RELATIONSHIP RAPPORT
MAY SOMETIMES REQUIRE
RELATIONSHIP REPAIR.

relationship

RELATIONSHIP (n.) - the way people relate to, connect and bond with each other

relationship

Hi! I'm glad you're here!
Oh! I love you too!
I'm really glad you care!

Thanks for always helping me.
I trust you. I can confide in you.
I really want our special relationship
to last and last and last.

Sometimes I feel so lonely!
I want someone special in my life
to love me, need me
and who really cares!

Why can't I find that person?
It seems so unfair.
I know there must be someone out there.
I will just have to keep on looking.
Thanks for listening!

Look at YOU?
Why?

Thoughts: Don't take others for granted

□rescue

**How foolish to believe
that you can rescue others
when YOU are also drowning.**

RESCUE (v.) - save someone from a
dangerous or difficult situation

rescue

You are drowning in a sea of problems
of your own making.

Unable to stand on the firm ground
of responsible choice,
you are being pulled away
by the strong undertow
of unshakable habit.

You resign yourself to go with the flow,
willingly accepting wherever it takes you
regardless of the consequences.

I see you are in trouble. I want to help.
I throw you a line and hold it tight.
You grab hold and pull yourself out.
You drop the line
and go off on your mission.

I lose my balance and fall in.
I am now in over my head.

You turn around and see me in trouble.
I'm still holding the line that pulled you out.
I shout for you to help me.
You turn and walk away
and never look back.

Here I am! Left alone to fend for myself
and wondering why I wanted to help you
without considering how to protect
and take care of myself first.

Thoughts: Trust carefully • Gratitude • Help yourself

RESPITE (n.) - a short break you are taking

respite

I'm weary of the dreary,
  and tired of being sad and brooding.
I'll adjust my range of feelings
  so a positive attitude can be exuding.

I'll smile for just a little while,
  and put on a happy face.
I'll think of the pleasant and upbeat
  just to change the pace.

I may not feel less serious
  or chase all the blues away,
but I can detour from my heavy mode
  and lighten my load for today.

So lift your spirits with a glint,
  a tune and a little giggle.
Look for nice and happy thoughts
  and give yourself a tickle.

It will pick you up and lift you out
  even if it may not last or stay.
For those few special moments,
  it will take you right away.

So if only for just a little while
  this lighter frame of mind
    will be a very welcome respite
      along the continuum of your time.

Thoughts: Make time for you • Joy & pleasure • Don't take things too seriously

☐ right

Know when you are on
the *wrong* side of
RIGHT!

People who assume
they are always right
usually aren't!

☐ rock-bottom

Rock-bottom
can be a good place to stand firm
and reach upward toward success.

☐ rudeness

Rudeness
is a weak man's imitation
of strength.

☐ rules

Conventional rules
are elastic guidelines
that keep us within tried-and-true boundaries
of safety.
They give with maturity and experience
to let us see how far
we can safely stretch our limits.

☐ run

Why run to me when you are in trouble
when you run past me when you are not?

RUN (v.) - quickly move away from; avoid

run

Can't you tell how I feel about you?
It's so hard for me to tell you I love you,
how much you mean to me and how much I care.
I just can't say the words.

I run away when you want me there.
I can't deal with seeing you troubled.
I care too much to know you are in pain.
I love you too much to see you hurting.

I can't bear the thought of you not being well.
I get angry when you're hurting.
I holler when you can't do what you always could.
I walk away scared when you want to tell me your fears.

Why? Maybe I'm so used to your strength and protection
that I can't transition to being the stronger one.
Maybe it's my way of being strong.

I cry when I realize that you may not
know how much I care,
see through my rough veneer or
realize I want to help but just don't know how.

Please understand! You always did!
You can't believe that I don't care anymore.
You can't think that I would leave you alone.

(continued)

You are in my heart and thoughts all the time.
I try to find ways to help.
I search for solutions.

Sometimes I think that maybe
I can best help by not being there.
Maybe others who are not so involved
can be more comforting and helpful.
But I'm always here caring, hoping and praying.

Please understand! I love you!

Thoughts: Don't judge others • You have limits

□ rut

Trying to help someone who doesn't want help
is like spinning your wheels in their rut.
You just get stuck with them in a trap that
holds both of you back from moving ahead.

☐sadness

Sadness
is an invisible millstone*
that weighs you down
and makes you unable to lift your spirits.
At times you forget it's with you,
but it still holds you back
from reaching as high as you could.

millstone: (figurative) - a heavy feeling or thing that weighs you down

sadness: A millstone

☐salt

Some people need to sprinkle salt on their food
BEFORE tasting it.
Others taste their food first
THEN sprinkle salt on if needed.
Curious!

☐save

What you $ave
You have!

SCARY-MOVIE (n.) - a movie that is frightening

Scary-movie

I went to see a movie
   with horror boldly advertised.
The place was filled with children
   from very small to big in size.

It had an okay rating
   so everyone could come.
There was no foul language
   or sex to turn them on.

The movie started with some screaming
   and someone being chased
by a crazy with a weapon
   who had lots of anger to waste.

People in the movie were
   cut, and hit and terrorized.
The audience was scared and screaming
   and at first even horrified.

The music and sound were very loud
   and punctuated every hurt.
The victims in the movie
   kept dropping in the dirt.

The story kept getting scarier.
   There were attacks of every kind.
The bloodier it got the better it seemed;
   the audience didn't mind.

Everyone watched intently
   as they ate their popcorn fast.
When more gruesome things happened,
   the giant sodas didn't last.

(continued)

Then the audience screams got fewer,
  and some laughs began to appear.
With each new horrible attack and hurt,
  the terror seemed to disappear.

The audience couldn't wait to see
  who got hurt the worst.
Folks focused on those who were able to escape
  to see when those feelings of safety burst.

The audience rooted for the villains
  and watched the innocents mowed down.
They cheered for those who did the hurting
  and laughed as the victims hit the ground.

The torture seemed like child's play
  to make it fun to watch on screen.
Screams from those hurt were always ignored
  by their attackers being mean.

The murder and the mayhem,
  the blood and gore and pain
and all the scared eyes and violence on screen
  went on and on in vain.

By now the audience watched gleefully
  as each violent act took place.
The color and music made everything seem
  more real in movie space.

It was hard to keep count of
  how much blood was spilled
or how many screen victims
  were hurt, in pain or killed.

As I watched these terrible things go on,
  I took some candy out.
I got a tiny paper cut.
  "Ouch, that hurt," I began to shout.

(continued)

I watched as actors on the screen
  were stabbed and punched and shot.
I couldn't really fully concentrate
  because my finger was hurting a lot.

I wondered if my wound could be serious,
  that paper cut I got.
After all, my pain felt terrible;
  a very nice thing it was NOT!

The movie ended with a scream.
  The lights came on. We got up and left.
Wasted popcorn and soda cups on the floor
  showed just how much we all had spent.

I'm sure the producers were happy
  at the screams and laughs they got.
But no one cared about my paper cut
  even though it still hurt me a lot.

I wondered for a little bit
  if those actors on screen ever healed.
Then I realized they weren't hurt AT ALL.
  Those awful wounds weren't even real.

Only we were the ones who really suffered
  watching this awful stuff.
Those scenes are now etched in our memories
  and will give us nightmares enough.

The movie gave its viewers
  lots of ideas on how cruel one can be.
It gave a view that when others are hurt,
  we don't have to care about what we see.

We all knew that what was on the screen
  wasn't real at all.
But my paper cut was different. *(It still hurt.)*
  It happened to ME after all!

(continued)

The vivid pictures, actions and mean words used
must of had writers spending lots of time
thinking up such awful ways to hurt others
so their movie could be fine.

Where did the writers get such violent thoughts
to inflict such pain and make it seem so real?
Maybe as children they watched scary-movies too,
and they never, *e-v-e-r* healed!

So maybe before children watch this awful stuff,
parents should be making a fuss,
since EVERYTHING we see and hear
does become a real part of us.

The people who inflict this on-screen horror
get paid a lot to make it look so bad.
Maybe they need a *'paper cut'* to remind them
that being hurt SHOULD make you sad!

Thoughts: Desensitizing • Reality vs. fantasy • Learning

scary movie: Reactions

SCUM (n.) - despicable people;
the lowest of the low

Scum

Is that you?
Contaminated by selfish motives?
Defiled by hurts?
Discarding trust and truth?
Excreting deceit?
Rotting in self-pity?
Stained by past rejections?
Foul? Offensive? Squalid? Unkempt?

It's time to change:
Rise above selfishness and self-gratification
by dressing yourself in courage.
Control the excretions of deceit
that befoul trust and truth.
Extricate yourself from the slime of exploiting
by ascending the ladder of perseverance.
Wash away the foulness of fears and frustrations
by cleansing yourself with self-belief.

Attract those who can help by:
Showering yourself with dignity.
Perfuming yourself with integrity.
Refreshing yourself with self-respect
and thoughtfulness.

Then look at yourself
in the mirror of reality!
THAT IS YOU!

Thoughts: Build self-image • Being down

SEED (n.) - flowering plant's way to reproduce

Seed

A seed, like each of us,
has a fragile and dependent beginning
as well as an extraordinary potential
to sprout, develop and flower.

To grow, a seed needs sustaining nourishment,
protection from damaging influences
and opportunities to uniquely bloom.

Seeds planted in non-nourishing soil and stuck in
shadows blocking the light of opportunity will
have a challenging path toward optimal growth.

Some seeds, even with the best of care,
may have results that are far less than hoped for,
while others, even in the most inhospitable
of environments, may be able to
fully grow and beautifully blossom.
Some seeds thought unable to even survive
will sprout, grow and bloom against all odds.

Determination, belief in self and the love of caring others
can make the difference.

Thoughts: Encourage growth • Persevere •
Give attention

seed: Sprouting

☐ self-control

Self-control

is a subtle self-harness

around the will

of one who accepts it.

☐ settle

Settle only for what
you CAN be
not just for what
you ALREADY are.

☐ sex

sex

SEX (n.) - sexual relations

Sex

Meeting
attraction
closeness
sharing
warmth
penetrating
breathless
exhilarating
Overwhelming
All concentrating
POWERFUL
Exhausting
Satisfying
touching
momentary
parting
cold
Over!

Thoughts: Coldness vs. warmth •
Lasting or momentary • Sex vs. love •
Physical vs. emotional love

☐shadows

Shadows appear

whenever we let darkness

push away light.

shadows

☐shell

Your shell
does keep hurt out.
It also keeps hurt in.

Source: P. 211

SHELL (n.) - hard outer cover with an opening

Shell

You have encapsulated yourself inside
  a thick shell to protect you from hurts sustained
    during your life – the failures, mistakes,
      lack of affection, loneliness and rejection.

Your shell isolates you from the world you see
  as cruel and uncaring and from those you feel
    may deceive or hurt you.

You allow no one to penetrate your shell.
  You suspect those, like the Trojan Horse gift,
    who show friendship and trust.
  You view affection and kindness as tools
    others may use to get the upper hand.
  Advice bounces off you like arrows off armor.

Your shell is real.
  To open it fully could make you vulnerable
    and an easy target for more hurt.
  To give of yourself could mean being used.
  To try and reach outside your shell could bring failure.
  To trust could bring betrayal.

When you must open your shell, it is just enough
  to set expectations low.
    You stubbornly refuse guidance.
    You accept momentary success rather than plan.
    You reach out to those who reject you
      rather than to those who could help.

Your shell blocks your vision of the beautiful and good.
  It seals in the heat of anger and distrust.

(continued)

Why open yourself to believe someone could really care
  when you were rejected by those you expected
    to give you affection and attention?
Why look to realizing your hopes and goals
  when you think you will fail?
Why trust when you feel so unworthy of trust?

Your shell does keep hurt out. It also keeps hurt in.

Open your shell
  before your shell smothers and destroys
    that which you are trying so hard to protect.

Thoughts: Imaginary shells • Purpose of a shell

shell

□should

If what should,
COULD
and what could,
WOULD
than what shouldn't,
WOULDN'T.

SLEEP (n.) - natural rest with little or no conscious thought

Sleep

You are at peace lying there with an angelic expression;
unafraid, oblivious, deep in your blissful sleep!

Your need for love and attention is put aside.
Your desire for someone to care and notice is forgotten.
Your love for those you consider special
lies powerfully still, deep in the recesses of your heart.

You dream of success, wealth and fame:
To have made it and be someone others can look up to.
To prove you could achieve to those who said you wouldn't.
To stand on your own two feet, head high, beholden to no one.
To block out having to accept indignities and being used.

Slowly, as the rays of reality begin to filter in,
you awaken to the new day.
The angelic smile begins to harden.
The bliss and peace of sleep begin to lift.
Your body stiffens to the demands that await you.
Your dreams condense to thoughts of the moment.
Your eyes narrow to the task ahead,
like blinders blocking out the light of self-respect.

Time to go after that quick means to your end.
Forget patience, perseverance and planning
toward a tangible and reachable goal.
It's too long. Use the minutes of your waking hours
in deliberate steps for short-range benefits only.

(continued)

Look in the mirror at your hardened features –
the deep frown, hunched walk, untrusting glances.
Listen to your surly voice and contempt for those succeeding
as you pursue your indifferent interactions.

Out you go into the world:
Hardened, cold, stubborn and uncaring.
Determined to get your limited goals.
Refusing to accept today as part of the future.

You spurn those who want to care,
drown out and ignore friendships and good advice,
lie to those who want to trust and
push away those who want to help.

You are an arrow shooting at an insignificant target –
too low, but using all your energy to reach it
leaving none to go further toward a distant goal.
With better aim in thought and determination,
you could reach a greater target leading to stability.

Back you come! Lonely, drained, unfeeling, empty.
Hopes and dreams damaged and unfulfilled.
Prepare for sleep.
Try to erase the thoughts of your deeds –
the rip-offs, the lies, the quick money.
Use whatever you need to make you forget.
Conceal the reality. Drown out the hurt.
Opiate the disappointment.

Sleep. Be at peace,
until you awake . . . .

*Thoughts: Sleep as escape • Wake up! •
Do rather than dream*

sleep

☐smart

**SO MANY PEOPLE
ARE TOO SMART
TO BE SO STUPID!**

☐smile, smiling

*Smile: A kiss of kindness
in an uncaring world.*

Smile: Warmth replacing cold.
Company after loneliness.
A sunburst through clouds
filling the whole of your perception
with light and good feeling.

**How much better it is
to stop CRYING
about what has passed
and start SMILING
about what could come!**

Source: P. 74 **(See P. 169)**

SPECIAL (adj.) - better, greater or different
from what is usual

Special

Each of us is SPECIAL,
each in our OWN way!
Each of us is DIFFERENT.
Who we ARE is okay!

Don't change to please others
who won't care anyway.
Stop worrying about what others
may or may not say.

If you want to be special,
seek out how you are unique.
Get help to develop it,
then give it your special tweak.

BELIEVE in yourself,
and others will believe in you too.
Others may see things in you
that YOU don't see in YOU.

Become the BEST YOU that YOU can be.
Be true to who you are.
That will help you feel special,
and you will go very far!

From Goldy and Friends and Their Amazing Adventure! ©2017

Thoughts: Self-confidence • Being unique

SPOTLIGHT (n.) - bright light that shines on a person on stage

Spotlight

Please shine your spotlight of attention on me
to keep me from being just one of the crowd.

I need to stand out as special,
magnified in importance,
as I do my act in the jazz beat
of my own rhythms – different, out there.

Shadow in the darkness to focus
only on what I want you to see
as I speak to everyone
but not allow anyone close enough
to see what's behind the role I'm playing.
Otherwise, you would know
what I really feel inside.

Being uncomfortable with myself,
I am unable to allow my inner glow
of feelings to reflect off others so they, too,
can shine in their own spotlight of attention.

Thoughts: Let others shine • Need for attention

□Spring

Spring

SPRING (n.) - warm season of the year; rebirth

Spring

The warm rays of Spring
  tweak out green shoots from Nature's dormant seeds
    as they reach out toward the blue sky
      eager to catch their share of the sun's rays.

Colorful blossoms pop forth.
  Yellows, reds and purples blanket stretches of green
    to herald the warm days ahead;
  pink and white clusters sway gently in the breeze.

The beautiful palette of nature's beautiful stars
  awakens our sense of awe,
  soothes us with lovely hues
  and entices us with delicious scents.

Give attention to the hues performing for us and see
  the rebirth and rejuvenation of the intricate blossoms.
Let the vibrant patches of color touch our innermost psyche
  and lift us out of Winter's stark coldness.
Heed the call of the flowers' powers signaling all is well.
Get ready to savor Spring
  by anticipating beautiful things to come.

We, too, can use our endless opportunity
  to bloom to our fullest potential
    and sense a oneness with nature's beauty.
Join with nature's *'Children of Spring'*
  as they perform for us and show us the way.

*Thoughts: Rebirth • Appreciate nature •
New beginnings*

STAR (n.) - famous or outstanding performer;
- successful person; celebrity

Star

song

In a lifetime, everybody needs
to Feel Important in some way.
Everybody likes to Be Recognized.

Everybody wants to Be
at the Center Stage of Attention some time.
Everybody wants to Take that Special Bow.

Everybody hopes to Shine
in the Spotlight of Life somewhere.
Everybody likes to Hear that Applause.

Everybody wants to Know
each is Special somehow,
and at least one time wants to Feel 'On Top.'

So at that time
LIFT THE CURTAIN!
SHINE THE SPOTLIGHT!
and START THE APPLAUSE!
because
Everybody needs to Shine.
Everybody likes that Bow.
Everybody wants to be a STAR!

Thoughts: Recognition • Feel appreciated • Self-image • Showcase talents • Be noticed • Stand out

star: In the spotlight

☐ start

The sooner you start,
no matter how small a step,
the sooner you'll be on your way.

Source: See P. 220

Start Smart!
End Ahead!

A step
is a start!

START (n.) - where something begins

Start

The long and arduous journey ahead
has no clear or easy road to follow:
The moving river is deep and frightful.
The ominous darkness blinds you
from seeing in front.
The rough path restricts you
from smooth going.
The treacherous pit awaits your fall.

So no matter when you start,
the long journey is still as arduous:
The moving river is still deep and frightful.
The ominous darkness is still blinding.
The rough path is still restrictive.
The treacherous pit still awaits your fall.

The sooner you start, no matter how small a step,
the sooner you'll be on your way and closer
to reaching your new and desired destination.
Why wait? START NOW!

Thoughts: Procrastination • Fear of beginning • Stuck

start: Dive right in!

STATUS-QUO **(n.) - staying the same; not changing**

Status-quo

You plant yourself firmly in the sands of habit:
Accepting whatever comes. Content with what is.
Unmindful of what could be.

You view your present circumstances as inevitable
rather than looking at what could be.

You wallow in the rut of past choices
and find refuge in the familiar.

You wear blinders to shield you
from options and opportunities.

You are willing to survive in your status-quo
rather than reach for ways to grow.

As the constant tides of time
slowly wash away the sands of possible change,
you sink deeper and deeper into the familiar
of your chosen consistent environment.

You are stuck
in your status-quo!

*Thoughts: Habit vs. change • Try new things •
Fear of & resistance to change*

□ stereotypes

Stereotypes
are frivolous distortions
emphasizing
the most offensive surface aspects
of what appears to be reality.

STOP **(v.) - cause an action, process or event to come to a halt or an end**

Stop

If you had stopped for a moment
to think where you were going,
maybe you wouldn't be where you are.

Stop!

If you had paused for a second
to look where you were headed,
maybe you'd be somewhere other than here.

Look!

If you hadn't moved so fast
and had listened to good advice,
maybe you could have made better choices.

Listen!

(continued)

If you had thought for an instant
to consider what you were doing,
maybe you would have done something else.

Think!

So if you stop for a moment
and change where you are headed
- and you definitely can! -
maybe you'll wind up
where you really want to be.

Change!

Thoughts: Consider options • Impulsivity • Get advice

□strangers

Two People,
just a word away.
Yet nothing passes
to bridge the gap of
ideas, interests, qualities
and thoughts.
Two Strangers, STILL . . . .

Why do we describe strangers
as *'perfect,'*
but see so many imperfections
in those we know well?

□strength

Your strength
lies not in your muscles
but in your inner qualities of:
Kindness.
Caring.
Giving of yourself.
Believing in me.

Source: P. 225

strength

STRENGTH (n.) - being strong, powerful, determined

Strength

You are strong!
I can lean on you,
and your confidence in me holds me up
in my time of weakness and frailty.

Your attention
electrifies me with warmth all over.

Your caring
shelters me from my fears like a protective cover.

Your kindness
melts away my frozen expression of sadness and fear.

Your presence
builds my courage and belief in myself.

Your words
soothe the roughness of my world.

Your strength
lies not in your muscles
but in your inner qualities of:
Kindness.
Caring.
Giving of yourself.
Believing in me.

You give me strength to go on
to face my problems,
to want to overcome.

Thoughts: Physical vs. character strength • Mentoring

Hard challenges can
reveal strengths we didn't know we had,
push us to find the solutions we seek
and build the emotional muscles
we need to persevere.

□stuck

Why do some repeatedly GIVE what they cannot afford
in order to GET what they definitely don't need
then wonder why they STAY STUCK where they don't want to be?

STUPID-QUESTION (n.) - a question someone rudely labels as ignorant, foolish or dumb

Stupid-question

Today I asked a question
about something I wanted to know.
You called my question *'STUPID,'*
but I don't think that's so!

I believed you would respond to me
in a kind and knowledgeable way.
Your answer was surprising,
and it really upset my day.
When you responded *"That's a stupid question,"*
I felt embarrassed and small.
Was I supposed to know the answer?
Or should I not have asked at all?

To get a correct answer,
I must ask those who should know;
but if they make that uncomfortable to do,
where else should I go?

(continued)

So if I want to understand
        but am discouraged and won't ask,
then finding out a correct answer
        becomes an impossible task.

So thinking about it further,
        perhaps the problem was not me.
My question wasn't stupid,
        your response just made it seem to be.
My question came from wanting to know
        something that I didn't.
So did your defensive action show
        it was something that YOU didn't?

I never got my answer
        because you never gave me one.
Instead you made it a contest of wits,
        and you thought you won.
You probably didn't have an answer
        or were caught in a mistake.
Or did my question touch a nerve in you
        triggering a defensive response to make?

So now when there's a question
        and I ask someone who should know,
if they would say *"It's stupid,"*
        I'll understand that doesn't make it so.

There are NO stupid questions
        that come from sincere folks.
Proper inquires should never be stifled
        with rudeness, sarcasm or jokes.
When I think about it further
        and about the person I asked it to,
I didn't have a stupid question at all.
        It seems the *'stupid'* one was YOU!

Thoughts: Value questions • Give careful responses

□succeed, success

What you succeed at may not be your choice.
What you try for is!

Success:
An attitude
not a possession.
An opportunity
not an end result.
Momentary,
not for all time.

How much better it would be to show those
who let your down,
who didn't believe in you,
who didn't give you a chance,
that you CAN succeed in spite of them.
Source: P. 74

Success at what you see as *EASY*
can satiate you and stop you from trying
for what you know is *DIFFICULT*.

success

SUCCESS (n.) - a favorable result; achieving

Success

An ABILITY: You demonstrate
what you can do.

An ACCOMPLISHMENT: You are able to shine
whether in the most significant of activities
or at the most minimal of tasks.
Others can look and say *"Well done!"*

An ACHIEVEMENT: You test limits, use skills
and talents to complete the task at hand.

An AWARENESS: You have a clear vision
of where you have been, where you are
and where you can grow further.

A CONFIDENCE: You know you can do well
and are willing to handle new challenges.

A FEELING: You have pride and satisfaction
In knowing YOU are able to achieve.

An OPPORTUNITY: You can build on
your continuum of directional preferences
and can be helpful to others still striving
for their first victory.

A SECURITY: You feel comfortable
at your new plateau of achievement
and can look toward more advanced ones.

A TALENT: Your achievement
Is now in your repertoire of skills.

A WILLINGNESS TO TRY: You believe in yourself
enough to go after what you want,
even if you may not always succeed.

Thoughts: Build on success • Willing to try • Look ahead

SUNSHINE (n.) - direct sunlight unbroken by clouds;
- cheerfulness, happiness

Sunshine

song

I'm sending a package
of sunshine
wrapped in a sky of blue.
It's tied with a rainbow ribbon
made especially for you.

On top there'll be
a big bouquet
of lovely Forget-Me-Nots,
and sprinkled over
with Four-Leaf Clover
just to wish you good luck.

Inside there'll be
a card of Gold
in the shape of a heart.
Inscribed will be
those special words,
I LOVE YOU!

sunshine: Forget-me-nots

SURVIVAL (n.) - continuing to exist and go on

Survival

You are in a battle for survival.

Courage: Drained by uncertainty.
You do only what you must to get by.

Feelings: Immobilized by hurt.
You act without belief, emotion or hope.

Hands: Chained by anger.
You grasp only at the immediate
without considering its value or harm.

Hearing: Clouded by doubt.
You disbelieve the good things you hear about
your ability, potential, quality and talents.

Legs: Shackled by lack of confidence.
You only take small steps in limited directions.

Mind: Dulled by desperation.
You think only of instant gratification.

Motivation: Imprisoned by self-imposed constraints.
You limit your efforts, thoughts and vision
to the simplest goals and resist the challenging.

Personality: Scarred by bad experiences.
You dare not allow yourself to trust
or get close to anyone.

Strength: Ebbed by lack of hope.
You do not challenge obstacles.

Vision: Blinded by past failures.
You do not allow yourself to see opportunities.

Will you be able to overcome,
or are you already a prisoner of your fear?

Thoughts: Overcome fear • Build self-confidence

SUSPECT (v.) - believe without proof
that others have bad intentions

Suspect (v.)

Some overly use past negative experiences
as radar alarms to signal danger
from the approach of anyone
who offers caring or trust.

Some unreasonably suspect:
Good intentions
as invasions of privacy.
Offers of friendship
as encroachments on independence.
Professions of love and acceptance
as attacks on the psyche.
Smiles and warmth
as possible deceptions.

If this is YOU, it may be time
to suspect YOUR suspicions!

Thoughts: Inability to trust • Low self-image

☐**tact**

Tact is the art
of getting the point across
without making others feel they've lost.

TAKE (v.) - get possession of; accept

take

Sure I took! Why shouldn't I?
You offered, didn't you?
So what if I didn't use what you gave
the way you wanted me to?
I didn't ask you to give.
I even told you not to.

You wanted me to have. You insisted!
Why should I turn down something for nothing?
If I didn't take, you'd give to someone else.
Why should I do without?
Why shouldn't I enjoy getting?

Give something back? Why?
I never said I would.
Do I appreciate?
I really don't think about it.
You gave. I took. That's all!

Why would you expect anything from me?
You gave because you wanted to.
I took because I wanted to.
We're even!

See you around!

Thoughts: Expectations • Greed • Taking advantage

TAPESTRY (n.) - expensive fabric woven with intricate designs; displayed to be admired

tapestry

You display your unique tapestry for all to admire.
  But what you display as your finished product
    is a worthless deception, a recycled facade
      made to appear genuine.

It can't be defended, only pitied.
  Its flaws are glaringly visible
    to anyone who observes carefully.
  It is designed to resemble truth, but
    incongruous pieces don't fit properly.
  Mismatched threads of lies
    enmeshed in a few golden strands of truth
      don't hold up and gradually unravel with wear.
  Subtle inconsistencies of tones conflict
    like discordant notes in an
      otherwise pleasing symphony.

Much effort was expended by others
  to help salvage something special
    from what was accepted as being
      hopelessly damaged and beyond repair.

Your workmanship created nothing lasting.
  The time, effort and skill used to deceive
    could have been productively used
      to make for real growth and change.

Perfection was not expected,
  but integrity of work in progress was.

(continued)

Those who lovingly invested
confidence, hope and trust in what they believed
could be a potential masterpiece
are left confused and dismayed
that someone who they believed in
would distort truth for gain.

Now only salvaged remnants of hope for growth
remain from what could have been
a precious keepsake to have been displayed
with pride by both those
who invested their interest and trust
and the receiver of their good intentions.

Thoughts: Integrity • Behavior patterns show

□ teacher

teacher

TEACHER (n.) - a person who teaches;
- one who instructs in a school

teacher

You are our children,
  but we are not your parents.

We guide, correct and watch you grow
  in interests, self-image and skills.

We provide you with experiences that
  challenge you to do your best,
  encourage you to try new things,
  strengthen your weaknesses.

We give our time, energy and talents
  to help, direct and care about you.

We watch and listen
  when you have something to show or tell.

We are there
  when you need someone to rely on.

We encourage, guide and praise you to
  become what we know you could be.

We are proud and hopeful at the outcome
  that we will probably never see.

We send you out
  for others to know
    the results of our efforts.

Thoughts: 'In loco parentis' • Influence

☐**tears** (n.)

Tears
dissolve the mask we wear
to hide hurt, disappointment and loss.
They clear us,
cleanse us,
release us
so we are ready to go on
to meet new challenges.

Source: See P. 238

tears

TEARS (n.) - drops of salty fluid from the eyes

tears

Tears have a tiny beginning.
There is no reservoir at the source,
but once released, the flow can be vast.

Tears are powerful.
They blur our sight and perceptions
preparing us to receive truth.
They dull the optimism of dreams
leaving us with a clearer vision of reality.
They wash away false hopes
that clog our ability to go on.

Tears dissolve the mask we wear
to hide hurt, disappointment and loss.
Tears make us focus our emotions.
They narrow the scope of our thoughts.
They demand intense concentration
on our pent-up and debilitating feelings.

Tears show us:
We have limits. We are vulnerable.
We are not invincible or all-powerful.
Tears signal to others:
We are in need. We are in pain.
We need comfort.

Tears clear us, cleanse us, release us
so we are ready to go on
to meet new challenges.

Thoughts: Repressing tears • Sadness & joy

TEDDYBEAR (n.) - soft stuffed toy; looks like a bear

teddybear

A lovable teddy bear
slightly shabby and worn.
Arms outstretched
and ready to give others
a warm and secure refuge
from their uncertain world.

It is cast in a role of:
Accepting what others want to do.
Being there to please
so others can be happy.
Listening to what others need to share.

Invisibly buried inside the perpetual smile
is a loving heart
also needing attention,
and an inaudible voice
that says *"I'm somebody too!"*

Thoughts: Comfort and security • Being a 'teddy bear'

□tense (n.)

Dreams
are FUTURE Tense.
Failure
is PAST Tense.
Work
is PRESENT Tense.

☐thinking

For some, *thinking*
is just a momentary tactic
to fill time
between impulsive reactions.

☐threat

SOME PEOPLE ARE A
THREAT
TO SOCIETY
WHILE OTHERS ARE A
TREAT.
WHAT A 'H---' OF A DIFFERENCE!

TIME (n.) - every moment

time

The sun comes up, and the new day begins.
Morning is fresh, alive and young.
It is filled with the promise and hope
of the new day ahead.
We are energized to tackle the tasks beginning.

As the sun rises and the heat of the day
beats down on us, we encounter easy goings at first
as well as delays, wrong turns and problems.
We move at our established speed
anticipating whatever awaits us.

As our pace slows, our horizons begin to close in.
Yet we are determined to keep going even though
the excitement of beginning has worn off.

(continued)

As time goes by, our perceptions change.
Anticipation becomes
coping with the unexpected.
Hoping and dreaming
become accepting the immediate reality.
The drive to do so much
becomes the need to do what we can.
Our vicarious, energetic and whimsical steps
become a steady cadence.

As evening gently arrives, a tired peace sets in.
We are thankful for the journey and its many encounters
that we can fondly remember and internalize.
We are even more thankful for the chance to rest –
away from the challenges, the frantic pace
and the problems that confronted us on the
trek that started what seems like so long ago.

Now weary, we pause and reflect on all that we did.
We are grateful for what pleased us,
somewhat disappointed at what escaped us
and acceptingly satisfied to be just where we are.

As time clears the path so the new can sprout and grow,
we watch those just starting out.
Their enthusiasm, energy and hope kindle in us
flashbacks of our youthful exuberance.

We perk up, if only in empathy,
yet pleased we do not have to
be out there beginning all over again.

(continued).

As we watch night slowly approach,
we hold back time for just a few more moments
savoring the brief flickers of light still in front of us
as we stay in the status quo for just a while longer.

Gradually we accept the end of our busy day
and retire to our earned inevitable peace and rest.

Those who love us see us nodding off.
They want to try to stop the natural course,
perhaps hopeful that the energy
of our attention will continue,
or to just hold onto their past a bit longer.

Night brings its inevitable darkness. But in the
darkness, we can look for the light of new beginnings –
the same light that was in every precious moment
we have been given all along.

Now, with earned anticipation, we await
the welcome of a new tomorrow.

Thoughts: Aging • Acceptance • Satisfaction • Beginnings

☐time-goes-by

time-goes-by

TIME-GOES-BY (phrase) - every moment as it happens

time-goes-by

We can aimlessly watch time go by:
Waiting, hoping and wondering where it went.

Or we can productively make it work for us by:
Chipping away at failures.
Climbing over fears.
Confronting problems.
Cutting though doubts.
Edging past troubles.
Untangling miscommunications.
Wearing away obstacles.

Time goes on! But go with it,
so when the hourglass is full, you will know
you have used your time to the utmost!

Thoughts: Progress • Accomplish • Be productive

☐today

ACCEPT TODAY,
BUT ADJUST, CONFRONT AND MODIFY IT
TO CREATE A COMFORTABLE NOOK
IN WHICH TO SURVIVE, COPE AND GROW.

Source: P. 244

Handle Today,
using your reservoir of Yesterdays,
while awaiting the potential
of your Tomorrows.

Source: See P. 244

Today is Yesterday's Tomorrow
and will be Tomorrow's Past.

**Today
is not forever!**

Today is made up of
our *Yesterdays* to build on
and our *Tomorrows* to build for.

TODAYS (n.) - the present; now; each day

todays

**Our todays
are delicate concoctions
of our yesterdays and our tomorrows:
Recollections from the past
and anticipations for the future.**

**Accept today,
but adjust, confront and modify it
to create a comfortable nook
in which to survive, cope and grow.**

**Handle today,
using your reservoir of yesterdays,
while awaiting the potential and hopes
of your tomorrows.**

Thoughts: Possibilities • Enjoy the present • Plan

TRAIN (n.) - railroad cars moved by a locomotive

train

The ticket states my destination.
  I board, and the journey is left in others' hands.

What will happen on the journey
  is open to chance:
    Who will I meet?
    Will there be detours?
    What experiences will I encounter?
    Will the schedule be kept?
    When I get to my planned destination,
      will it be what I expected?

Perhaps where I am going is not as important
  as what I make of the journey along the way.

Perhaps my stated destination
  isn't where I really need to get to at all.
    Maybe I just need to enjoy the ride!

ALL ABOARD!

Thoughts: Where are you headed? • On the right track? • Enjoy the ride • Be open to experiences

train: Ticket

TRAIN-TRIP (n.) - going somewhere by train

train-trip

I'm sad. I have to go to a funeral.
  It will be a long trip, but I have to go.
Oh, well! Here's the train.
  I'll find a quiet seat so I can close my eyes and rest.

Oh, No! Children!
  I hope they have the manners to be quiet
    and let me shut out the world.
We're on our way now. It will be a long trip.
  I'm glad I brought a book to read.

"Oh, Daddy! Look at the beautiful flowers out there."

Huh? What? Oh, I guess I nodded off.
  What's that noise?
  Flowers? I don't see any flowers.
  What are they talking about?
  Don't those kids know how to be quiet?

"Look Mom, see those beautiful horses?"
  the children called out.
"Oh, there's a little one.
  That must be his brother that he's playing with.
  Look! They are all running and playing. So cute."

More noise! Can't their parents make them stop?
  I'm trying to rest. I have a sad day ahead of me.

"Look, wheat fields as far as I can see," one child said.
  The children pressed their faces up against
    the train window to see.

(continued)

The older one told the younger one,
"They grind wheat to become the flour.
That's what bread is made from.
Cake, cookies and cereal are made from the flour.
Wow! Look at all that wheat! It's so beautiful."

Don't they ever stop?
Just when I get my eyes closed, they start up again.
Maybe I should change my seat. Hum, all filled!
I guess I'll just turn over and try to rest.

Now what! Oh! We're slowing down.
We're going over an old bridge.

"Oh, look! A river," the children said excitedly.
"There are fishermen. It looks like one caught a fish!
See the birds! Aren't they beautiful? So many of them!
Wow! A deer! It's a whole family! They are so pretty."

"Look! There's a small town coming up," one child said.
"I see houses and roads and cars.
That looks like a circus tent! Is that a Ferris wheel?
Oh, Daddy! Can we go to the circus some time?
I like the clowns and acrobats. It's such fun.
Do you think they have cotton candy?
Isn't the sun bright and beautiful? This trip is great!"
The children pressed their faces close to the window.

Okay! I've had it! I should tell the parents
to teach their children some manners.
Why don't they have a book for them to read
or just tell them to keep quiet? That sun!
I'll pull down the shade so I don't have to see it.

(continued)

I guess it won't be much longer.
Another hour of this and I can get off.
I guess someone will meet me.
I hope they aren't too upset.
I hope I don't cry. What a sad trip!

Well, here we are! I'll just get my bags and get off.
Oh, that family is getting off too.
The children are running to greet someone. Such hugs!
The children are telling them all about the trip.
They are all smiling and laughing!
What's that they are saying? How they do go on!
The beautiful wheat fields, the horses,
the fishermen and circus tents?
They are so happy and excited about what they saw.
I guess they can't understand how sad a trip can be.
When they grow up, they'll realize how important it is
to not distract others with all that stuff.

Well, off to the funeral. I'm glad I got SOME rest!
Those children! I hope they learn some manners soon.

Thoughts: Perspective • Youthful exuberance

train-trip: Perspective

☐travel

Some shut out what they see along their way,
while others open their eyes wide
to take in everything they can.

TREASURE (n.) - person or thing valued; precious

treasure

The Old Coin:
Tarnished, dulled, bent. ***Discarded!***
The Rolled-up canvas:
Peeling, dirty, cracked. ***Unused!***
The Dusty Book:
Beat up; pages creased. ***Unread!***
The Rejected Person:
Alone, discouraged, sad. ***Ignored!***

But look closer!
The Old Coin: ***Valuable and Rare!***
Slips by time unnoticed.
The Rolled up Canvas: ***A Masterpiece!***
Undiscovered and unrecognized for what it is.
The Dusty Book: ***Priceless!***
Left to mildew and deteriorate.
The Rejected Person: ***Feeling and Loving!***
Lost and alone.

Unique treasures all!
Innate worth unrecognized unless examined closely.
Intrinsic value disguised, hidden, unknown
or not understood. (continued)

Learn to discover what is not evident at first glance.
Peel away the scars of age, rejection and use.
Reclaim what appears damaged and worthless.
Recognize potential and innate quality.
Reveal the beautiful essence, quality and good.
Invest time, effort, attention and love
to discover the treasures in each individual
no matter how deeply hidden or disregarded.
Remove the encrusted pain of neglect and
restore what has been overlooked!

Always look for the good in others,
not just at how good others look.
Appreciate the quality you discover in others
that may not be understood at first glance.

And as you search for the treasure in others,
don't overlook those hidden qualities
within yourself, the treasures you too possess!

Thoughts: Hidden potential • Caring •
Respect for others

☐ tree

tree

Father Tree
rooted in Mother Earth
reaches to God's Heaven.

Source: P. 251

TREE (n.) - tall, woody plant with a trunk,
branches and leaves

tree

Father Tree
rooted in Mother Earth
reaches to God's Heaven.

It provides a fence of security and beauty
in an otherwise bland landscape, protecting against
the world rushing in unobstructed.

It is home to a population
of birds, squirrels and insects that scatter through.

Wandering roots seek their most secure spot
to firmly anchor their lofty entity
and take up needed nourishment
so it can freely grow.

Green leaves strategically blanket its branches
to capture sunlight in their magical pockets
while providing needed shade below.

Trees make the air fresh, the ground fertile,
provide food, shelter, protection and shade
for those that depend on it
and stand as a majestic parent
to the awe-inspired family of man.

Thoughts: Majesty of trees • Importance of trees

□truth

TRUTH for some
becomes the weapon of last resort.
It is only considered
when no other viable options exist.
Even then, its use is calibrated
in the smallest measure possible.

TRUTH (n.) - honesty; accurate information

truth

Truth is an invisibly fine golden chain:
Exquisitely crafted. Preciously beautiful.
It separates the world of reality
from a world of deception and confusion
and brings forth a bright sunshiny inner glow
of integrity and trust in those that use it.

Truth requires neither backup stories
nor the burden of remembering
so as not to contradict itself.

Truth is a powerful purge.
It clears the conscience and frees us to:
Accept others at face value.
Perceive objectively.
React from the heart.
See beauty and good.

Truth is an accomplishment of credibility
and a gift of openness and peace of mind.
It links us to reliable others
who WE can believe in, depend on and trust
and who can believe in, depend on and trust US.

Thoughts: Truth as a way of life • Truth vs. lying

TURN-it-AROUND (v.) - change direction, attitude

turn-it-around

song

When the world gets you down,
just pick yourself up and turn it around.
Turn it around.

When the world shuts you out,
come on back in and turn it around.
Turn it around.

When the world seems gloomy,
paint a rainbow above.
Just stick out your chin, let the sunshine come in
and turn it around.
Turn it around.

If the world turns you off,
just switch yourself on
and turn it around.
Turn it around.

When you think it's the end,
put a smile on your face
and start all over again.

When nothing seems to go right,
just stop where you are.
Take a stand and say *"It's a brand new day,"*
and just turn it around.

So believe you can turn the world your way.
Make today your own special day,
and turn it around.

JUST TURN IT AROUND!

☐understand

I understand you,
because I see in You, Me!

☐uses (v.)

Anyone who uses me loses me!

☐used-to

We get used to
what we get used to.

VALUE (n.) - importance or worth of something

Value

Sometimes simple common things and seemingly
insignificant deeds can become really important
if and when we are in need.

Tangibles: Those things *we* can touch and feel
become essential when the need is real.

GASOLINE: Some processed oil for a car or truck.
If we run out, we're really out of luck.

KEY: A small piece of metal with notches more or less.
It's the difference between having shelter
and being locked out in a mess.

(continued)

LIFE JACKET: A simple piece of plastic
filled with lots of air.
It's a life-saving difference,
but only if there is one to wear.

PENCIL: A long piece of graphite
inside some colorful wood.
If it's there when we need it, we'll remember
important things we should.

Intangibles: What we can't see or touch
can still make a big difference for us.

CARING: A special attitude of giving
that offers all of us hope.
It provides us with important needed strength
to help us to be able to cope.

KINDNESS: Simple gestures and little acts
so very easy to do. *They bring smiles and*
good feelings when shared with others and you.

PROMISE: Important words to sincerely apply.
When honestly given, they are strong enough
on which we can all rely.

SMILE: A simple facial expression that we've all got.
Even just a little bit can warm our world a lot.

WORDS: Just little puffs of beaten air.
They make it possible to communicate and share.

So realize even little things given by those who care
can be of significant value but only
if available and there.

Thoughts: Insignificant vs. significant •
Making a difference

VENEER (n.) - an attractive covering to disguise something's true nature

Veneer

To appear perfect, untroubled
and able to handle whatever may come:
We clothe ourselves
to look uncaring and unaffected.

We erect emotional barriers
to conceal our innermost thoughts and feelings.

We make up with control and aloofness
to hide loneliness and insecurity.

We put on carefree masks
to project the image we want seen.

We show our strengths
so our limitations cannot be discovered.

Our veneer does cover what we want to hide:
We can look strong on the outside
even if we feel wanting inside.

We can block others from realizing
when we are in need of their help,
support and caring.

So nothing really changes!

Thoughts: Looks can be deceiving • Why hide feelings?

☐victim

The Evil prey on the vulnerable
and *the Selfish* take from the giving.
Neither cares for their victims,
nor gives more than they must
to achieve personal gain.

W, Y *Pp. 257-267*

☐walls

**Some of us build walls
so others can't get in;
while others build walls
so they don't have to get out.**

☐want

Sometimes,
what we WANT
may not be
what we SHOULD HAVE!
Want Wisely!

WANT (v.) - feel a need; crave, desire, hope for

Want

I want what I want when I want it!
Why won't you do what I want?
It makes me happy to have things my way!
I wouldn't expect if I didn't want what I ask for.

So you want your way, too?
Oh! I guess that's all right!
Why shouldn't you have what you want?
It would be nice, even great,
if everyone had their way.
That's what should be!

But what happens if what I want
stops you from getting what you want,
or it displeases you, or puts you out
or conflicts with what you want?
Hum! Well, that's too bad!
Maybe YOU can change!

What happens if what you want
stops me from getting what I want,
or doing what I like or getting my way?
That's bad! I wouldn't want that!

Thoughts: Being selfish • Needs vs. wants

☐warming

Kindle the buried flame in others
by igniting your own spark
and warming the world around you.
Source: P. 33

☐ weeds

If you look in the weeds,
  don't expect to find exotic blossoms.

WILD-STALLION **(n.) - untamed adult male horse in the wild**

Wild-stallion

A majestic wild stallion
  stations himself in full view for others to admire.
A free spirit running with the wind,
  he swiftly, deftly and with grace
    finds his way alone.

Without clear goals or commitments,
  he runs in any direction that
    pleasure, need or fear takes him.

Whenever the urge to move calls,
  he gallops on paths of his own choosing
    encountering confusing wildernesses,
      turbulent rivers and desolate plains.

Without reins and refusing to be led or restrained,
  he is always just out of reach of anyone
    who could steer him away from danger
      or toward greener pastures.

Disregarding consequences, this loose spirit
  unknowingly crosses boundaries and jumps
    the conventional fences of society's norms.

(continued)

Along the way, he encounters others equally untamed
to run with him and gives these new companions
the caring, acceptance and kindness
that he refuses to seek for himself.

Head held high, he self-confidently senses that the
far-off horizon holds security, peace and fulfillment.
But running only in the darkness of instinct and ignorance,
he is unable to blaze a meaningful trail
toward any lasting goal.
At times he moves in dead-end circles making his
trail to the future a rut that keeps him stuck in the past.

This loose spirit bears the scars and wounds
of impetuous moves, vicarious habits and
painful experiences that he could have avoided
had he let trail-experienced others guide him.

Now stalked by inevitable growth and experience,
he responsibly narrows his choices
to more direct, restrained and stable roads.

As the new day dawns and maturity takes hold,
the light of conventional habits and reasonable limits
reveal a secure and peaceful path ahead.

Calculated choices with meaningful goals in sight
gradually replace aimless meanderings and poor choices.
Obligation and responsibility finally replace whim and desire.

Tame!

Thoughts: Impulsiveness • Maturity • Wild vs. tame

□ **winner**

Winner . . . .
Able to accept what comes
and make it work for you.

Source: See P. 263

winner

WINNER (n.) - one who wins, achieves, succeeds

Winner

A winner is one who:

Adds to rather than subtracts from
the good of the world.

Believes that things can work out,
and only how and when are the variables.

Builds bridges not always knowing
if they will ever be used.

Changes worry to action,
disappointment to determination,
failure to new efforts,
mistakes to learning,
potential to productivity.

Creates strong foundations of trust.
Hopes when it seems useless.
Learns when its value is unclear.
Looks ahead not backwards.
Tries when it seems futile.

Makes his light shine as brightly as it can
using all the power he possesses.

Throws out lines not always knowing
if or where they will attach.

Turns disadvantage into advantage,
detours into new and exciting adventures,
obstacles into stepping stones
and problems into challenges.

(continued)

Views insurmountable barriers as plateaus from which to see things objectively.

Understands that life is made worthwhile by appreciating, helping others and being considerate and kind.

Being able to accept what comes and make it work for you!

Thoughts: Be positive • Learn from experience • Have confidence

☐ word

Your word is invisible, intangible and
gone as soon as it is uttered.
But once given, it is
indelible, invincible and unforgettable
to those who count on it.

Source: See P. 264

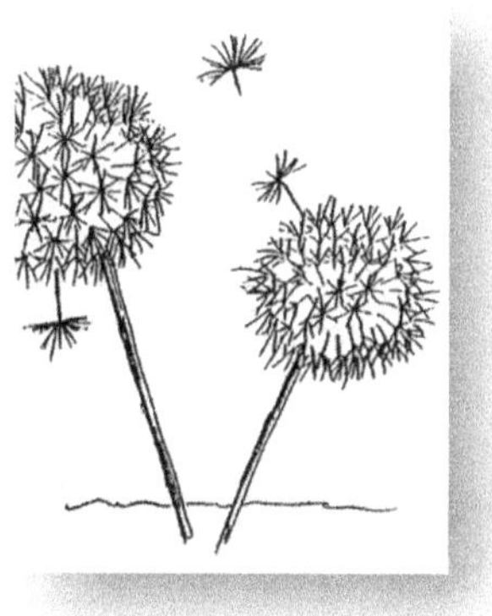

word: A ripe dandelion in the wind

WORD (n.) - what someone says, writes, promises

Word

When responsible, your word
  extends you to others with a strong invisible bond.
When irresponsible, it is:
  A commitment written in sand.
  Water in a cracked vessel.

Your word is either:
  A pledge to be kept or a loan left unpaid.
  A promise to be counted on or a bond to be broken.
  A trust to be upheld or a facade with no backing.
  A truth open for all to see or a whitewash to conceal.

Your word is a ripe dandelion in the wind,
  invisible, intangible and gone as soon as it is uttered.
But once given, it is indelible, invincible
  and unforgettable to those who count on it.
Your word is the foundation on which
  others build their image of your character.

Your word is *YOU!*

*Thoughts: Integrity • Mean what you say •
Reliability • Trust*

□words

Unkind words are *paper darts.*
  They can neither pain nor wound.
They hurt only if we let them penetrate our ego
  by lowering our belief in ourselves.

Source: See P. 157

Words designed to hurt?
I hear you, but I won't listen!

Source: P. 157

Your words have the power
to lift unbearable burdens.

Source: P. 182

WORDS
are nice
DEEDS
are better!

WORDS (n.) - something one uses to say or write;
- part of language

Words

Words can be deviously used as
strategic weapons in an arsenal of tools to:
Deflect detection of insincerity.
Extract what is wanted.
Gain entree to confidence.
Penetrate caution and trust.

Words can be purposely chosen
to strike with maximum power.

(continued)

Words can be aimed with feigned sincerity
and embellished with calculated emotion.
They can ease emerging doubts
in an unsuspecting target.

Words can be wielded as distracting time-fillers.
They can be used to avoid invasive inquiries
and be obstacles to meaningful communication.

Remember where words come from!
Words come from those who choose to speak them.

Listen and evaluate carefully!

Thoughts: Verify • Examine motives

□world

The world is like a mirror.
How you look at it
determines what it reflects back.

See image, P. 189

□youth

youth

YOUTH (n.) - young; not fully grown; not mature

Youth

Blunt
Realism and Common Sense.

Develop
Self-gratification and Self-indulgence.

Educate
with Drivel.

Emphasize the
Garish, Loud, Outward Appearance.

Ignore
Courtesy, Dignity and Respect.

Nourish
with Garbage.

Remove
Restraints.

Stunt Energy
by Passivity.

Surround
with the Ugly.

Varnish
Truth.

Then sit back
and Watch what develops!

Thoughts: Provide a good foundation •
Youth is the time to learn

Appendix: CONTENTS

M Pp.142-156

N - O Pp. 157-166

P Pp. 166-187

R Pp. 188-199

S Pp. 199-232

T Pp. 232-253

U, V, W, Y Pp. 254-267

www.ingramcontent.com/pod-product-compliance
Lightning Source LLC
LaVergne TN
LVHW050613100826
845148LV00011B/1567

* 9 7 8 1 7 7 1 4 3 4 1 8 8 *